THE RUSSIAN REVOLUTION AND SOVIET UNION 1910–91

GCSE Modern World History for Edexcel

Steve Waugh
John Wright

Hodder Murray

This high quality material is endorsed by Edexcel and has been through a rigorous quality assurance programme to ensure that it is a suitable companion to the specification for both learners and teachers. This does not mean that its contents will be used verbatim when setting examinations nor is it to be read as being the official specification – a copy of which is available at www.edexcel.org.uk.

The Publishers would like to thank the following for permission to reproduce copyright material:

Photo credits
p.6–9 David King Collection; **p.11** © Getty/Hulton; **p.12** *l* David King Collection, *r* © Corbis/Chris Hellier; **p.13** David King Collection; **p.14** *t* RIA-Novosti, *b* David King Collection; **p.15** David King Collection; **p.18** RIA-Novosti; **p.20–25**; David King Collection; **p.26** *l* David King Collection, *r* RIA-Novosti; **p.29** *t* © Corbis/Hulton-Deutsch, *b* David King Collection; **p.31** © Getty/Hulton; **p.32–34** David King Collection; **p.36** Popperfoto; **p.38–42** David King Collection; **p.46** RIA-Novosti; **p.48–61** David King Collection; **p.62** © Corbis/Hulton-Deutsch; **p.65** © Corbis; **p.66–69** David King Collection; **p.73** © Getty/Hulton; **p.74** © Network/Alex Chusonov; **p.77** *both* David King Collection; **p.78** *both* David King Collection; **p.79** *all* David King Collection; **pp.80–90** David King Collection; **p.92** © Network/Alex Chusonov; **p.94** Internationaal Instituut voor Sociale Geschiedenis, Amsterdam; **p.95–98** David King Collection; **p.100–101** RIA-Novosti; **p.102–107** David King Collection; **p.110** © Topfoto; **p.111–122** David King Collection; **p.123** © Corbis/Bettmann; **p.128** © Popperfoto; **p.129** RIA-Novosti; **p.131** © Corbis; **p.133** ©Andrzej Krauze 1990/The Guardian; **p.134** *l* RIA-Novosti, *r* © Topfoto; **p.135** © Getty Images; **p.136** © The Daily Telegraph 1980; **p.137** *l* © Rex Features/Sipa Press, *r* © Corbis/Bettmann; **p.138** © Corbis/Bernard Bisson & Thierry Orban/Sygma; **p.141** *l* RIA-Novosti, *r* © Corbis; **p.142** © Sipa Press/Rex Features; **p.143** *tl* © Getty Images/Chris Niedenthal/Time & Life Pictures, *b* © Topfoto, *tr* © Rex Features/Sipa Press; **p.144** *tl* © Corbis/Peter Turnley, *m* © Getty Images/Chris Niedenthal/Time & Life Pictures, *bl* © Corbis/ Bernard Bisson/Sygma, *r* © Corbis/Sophie Elbaz/Sygma; **p.146** *l* RIA-Novosti, *r* © Corbis/Bernard Bisson/Sygma.

Acknowledgements
p.7, 75 and 76 Edexcel Limited, June 2004 GCSE Modern World History paper; **p.11, 18, 22, 30, 31, 33, 36, 52, 70, 83, 89, 94, and 96** T. Fiehn, *Russia and the USSR*, Hodder Murray, 1996; **p.14, 30, 46, 48, and 51** T. Pimlott, *Russian Revolution*, Macmillan, 1985; **p.15** *l*, 27, 32, 41, and 54 J. Robottom, *Russia in Change 1870–1945 Modern Times*, Pearson Education Limited, 1984; **p.15** *r*, 31, and 33 J. Shuter, *Russia and USSR 1905–56*, Heinemann, 1996; **p.17** M. Brown, *Russia and Revolution*, Blackie; **p.18, 25, 35, 44, 45, 59, 60, and 61** J. Simkin, *The Russian Revolution*, Spartacus; **p.23 and 126** Evans and Jenkins, *Years of Russia and the USSR 1851–1991*, Hodder Murray; **p.24, 39, 71, 72, 73, 88, 92, 115, and 119** J. Laver, *Russia and the USSR 1905–56*, Hodder Murray, 1997; **p.36** Lynch, *Russia 1881–1924*, Hodder Murray; **p.39 and 67** J. Brooman, *Russia in War and Revolution*, Pearson Education Limited; **p.51** R. Pipes, *The Russian Revolution*, copyright © 1990 by Richard Pipes. Used by permission of Alfred A. Knopf, a division of Random House, Inc.; **p.61, 62, 63, 95, and 129** R. Radway, *Russia and the USSR 1900–95*, Stanley Thorne Publishers; **p.63 and 72** M. Lynch, *Russia: Reaction and Revolutions*, Hodder Murray; **p.67** C. Baker, *Russia 1917–45*, Heinemann; **p.80** Kelly, *Russia and the USSR 1905–56*, Heinemann, 1996; **p.85, 141 and 146** B. Walsh, *Modern World History*, Hodder Murray, 1996; **p.104** Freda Utley, *Lost Illusion*, 1949; **p.108** T. Downey, *Russia and the USSR*, Oxford University Press, 1996; **p.109** *l* T. Pimlott, *Stalin's Russia*, Macmillan; **p.109** *r* Kravchenko, *I Chose Freedom*, 1946; **p.121** Brooman, *Stalin and the Soviet Union*, Pearson Education Limited; **p.122** M. McCauley, *Stalin and Stalinism*, Pearson Education Limited; **p.124** J. Hasler, *The Making of the Soviet Union*, Pearson Education Limited; **p.127** D. Warnes, *Russia – A Modern History*, Hyman; **p.130** *t* A. White, *Russia and the USSR*, Collins. Reprinted by permission of HarperCollins Publishers Ltd.; **p.130** *b* W. Taubman, *Khrushchev*, Free Press; **p.131** M. Lynch, *Stalin and Khrushchev*, Hodder Murray; **p.139** MacDonald, *Russia and the USSR*, Pearson Education Limited; **p.140** Sauvain, *Key Themes of the Twentieth Century*, Nelson, 1996.

Every effort has been made to trace all copyright holders, but if any have been inadvertently overlooked the Publishers will be pleased to make the necessary arrangements at the first opportunity.

Orders: please contact Bookpoint Ltd, 130 Milton Park, Abingdon, Oxon OX14 4SB. Telephone: (44) 01235 827720. Fax: (44) 01235 400454. Lines are open 9.00 – 5.00, Monday to Saturday, with a 24-hour message answering service. Visit our website at www.hoddereducation.co.uk

Cover photo *l* © Dean Conger/Corbis; *r* David King Collection
Typeset in by Fakenham Photosetting Limited, Fakenham, Norfolk
Printed in Italy

A catalogue record for this title is available from the British Library

ISBN-10: 0 340 88902 0
ISBN-13: 978 0340 88902 2

Contents

Introduction

This book covers the key developments in Russia from 1910–91. Throughout the course you will learn about the following:

- Rasputin, a mad monk whose death was both unusual and controversial. Did the British Secret Service kill him?
- One of the most influential events of the twentieth century, the Bolshevik Revolution of 1917.
- The assassination of Tsar Nicholas II and his family. Did his daughter Anastasia survive?
- One of the bloodiest wars of the century – the Russian Civil War of 1918–21.
- The purges in Russia of the 1930s, which probably caused the death of millions.
- The amazing events of the late 1980s, which saw the break-up of the Soviet Union.

About the course

During this course you must study two outline studies, two depth studies and two coursework units. There are two written exam papers:

- In Paper 1 you have two hours to answer questions on two outline studies.
- In Paper 2 you have one and three quarter hours to answer questions on two depth studies.

Outline studies (Paper 1)

Outline studies cover a relatively long period of change and development. For example:

- Developments in the USA, from the US entry into the Second World War, in 1941, to the 1970s and the incredible events of Watergate during the presidency of Nixon.
- Key events in the Cold War, from the end of the Second World War to 1991. How close did the world come to nuclear war?

In this book you will study one of these outline studies – *The Rise and Fall of the Communist State:*

The Soviet Union, 1928–91. Chapters 7–11 give you the key information to ensure you are thoroughly prepared for this section and make judgements on the following issues:

- Why Stalin, a rank outsider to succeed Lenin, had emerged as leader by 1928 and why he introduced a massive programme of economic change including collectivisation and five-year plans.
- Why Stalin was responsible for the death of millions of Soviet citizens during his purges of the 1930s.
- Why Khrushchev, who succeeded Stalin in 1955, denounced Stalin and then tried even more extreme reform.
- How the Soviet Union stagnated under Brezhnev who, it is rumoured, was clinically dead in the last years of his period as leader.
- Why Gorbachev's two major reforms of the late 1980s, *Glasnost* and *Perestroika*, failed and brought about the collapse of the Soviet Union in 1991 and his own fall from power.

Paper 1 is very much a test of:

- knowledge and understanding of the key developments in each outline study
- the ability to write brief and extended essay-type questions.

In the examination you have to write brief and more extended essays, which ask you to demonstrate the following historical skills:

- Causation – why something happened.
- Consequence – the effects or results of an event.
- Change – how much change took place and why the change happened.
- Describe – a detailed description usually of the key events in a given period.

Chapters 7–11 give you detailed guidance on how best to approach and answer the types of question that you will be asked in Paper 1.

Depth studies (Paper 2)

Depth studies give you the opportunity to study a much shorter period in greater depth. For example:

- Nazi Germany, 1930–39 – Hitler's rise to power and the creation of the Nazi state in the years before the outbreak of the Second World War.
- The USA in the period 1929–41 – why US prosperity came to a sudden end in 1929, the impact of the depression that followed and Roosevelt's New Deal.
- The War in Vietnam, 1963–75 – how and why the USA became involved, and why it had such a devastating effect on both the USA and Vietnam.

Chapters 1–6 cover the key information and skills needed for *The Russian Revolution, c 1910–24* which is a popular depth study. It is often studied alongside the Soviet Union outline study.

Paper 2 is a test of:

- knowledge and understanding of a shorter period in history
- the ability to answer four different types of source questions.

In order to answer Paper 2 questions successfully, you need to have generic and question-specific source skills:

- 'Generic' means your ability to examine the nature, origins and purpose of sources.
- 'Question-specific' refers to the four different types of source questions. These are:
  - inference
  - cross-referencing
  - utility
  - the ability to discuss an interpretation.

Chapters 1–6 give you detailed guidance on how best to approach and answer these types of questions, and help you to gradually build up the source skills you need.

About the book

This book is divided into two main sections:

- The first section covers the depth study: *The Russian Revolution, c 1910–24.*
  It includes an introduction explaining the key areas of knowledge and understanding and the generic source skills. It is then divided into six chapters, which cover the main events and contain activities to develop, step-by-step, the specific source skills you need.
- The second section covers the outline study: *The Rise and Fall of the Communist State: The Soviet Union, 1928–91.*
  It includes an introduction explaining the key themes and areas of knowledge and understanding. It is then divided into five chapters, which give you detailed knowledge about each of these themes and contain activities to help develop, step-by-step, the exam skills you need.

Each chapter in this book:

- contains activities – some help develop the historical skills you need, others are exam-style questions which give you the opportunity to practise exam skills
- gives step-by-step guidance, model answers and advice on how to answer particular question types
- defines key terms and highlights glossary terms in bold the first time they appear in the outline and depth study sections.

The Russian Revolution, c 1910–24

Source A: **Starving peasants trading in human flesh in 1921**

This depth study tries to explain how the alarming events in the photograph above could have come about, by examining the reasons for the fall of the tsar in 1917, the success of the Bolshevik Revolution in the same year and the nature of the Bolshevik government, which ruled Russia under Lenin from 1917–24. Each chapter explains a key issue and examines a key line of enquiry as outlined below.

Chapter 1 Russia before the First World War (pages 9–16)
- Why was Russia so difficult to govern?
- How was Russia ruled?
- Why was Nicholas II such a weak tsar?
- Why was the economy so backward?
- Why were so many people unhappy?

Chapter 2 Opposition to tsarist rule (pages 17–26)
- Why was there a revolution in 1905?
- What did the political parties believe?
- Why were the *dumas* unsuccessful?
- Why did discontent grow from 1906–14?

Chapter 3 The impact of the First World War on Russia (pages 27–34)
- What was Russia's involvement in the First World War?
- Why did Russia suffer so many defeats?
- What effects did these defeats have?
- What were the effects of the war?

Chapter 4 Russia in 1917 (pages 35–44)
- Why was there a revolution in Russia in February 1917?
- What were the successes and failures of the Provisional Government?

Chapter 5 The nature of the Bolshevik takeover (pages 45–56)
- How did the Bolshevik Party strengthen?
- What was the role of Lenin?
- What was the role of Trotsky?
- What were the main events of the Bolshevik Revolution?
- Why were the Bolsheviks successful?

Chapter 6 Bolshevik rule and its impact, 1918–24 (pages 57–73)
- How did the Bolsheviks secure control?
- Why was the Constituent Assembly dissolved?
- Why was the Treaty of Brest-Litovsk important?
- Why did a civil war break out in 1918?
- Why did the Bolsheviks win the civil war?
- Why was War Communism important?
- What was the New Economic Policy?

Depth study questions

In the examination you will be given six sources and have to answer four questions. Here are the questions on this depth study for the June 2004 exam.

This is an **inference** question. This means getting a message or messages from the source.

This is a **utility** question – you must decide how useful a source is.

EXAM

PAPER 2

The Russian Revolution and Soviet Union Depth Study

(a) Study Source A.

What can you learn from Source A about the effects of the Russian offensive of July 1917 on the Russian soldiers?

(4 marks)

(b) Study Sources A, B and C.

Does Source C support the evidence of Sources A and B about the effects of the First World War in 1917 on the Russian troops? Explain your answer.

(6 marks)

(c) Study Sources D and E.

How useful are these two sources as evidence of the importance of Lenin's return to Russia in April 1917?

(8 marks)

(d) Study all the Sources.

'The main reason for the collapse of the Provisional Government in 1917 was the work of Lenin and the Bolsheviks'.

Use the sources and your own knowledge to explain whether you agree with this view.

(12 marks)

(Total 30 marks)

This is a **cross-referencing** question. It asks you to compare the views of three sources.

This is a **synthesis** question. It asks you to use the sources and your own knowledge to discuss an interpretation.

You will be given step-by-step guidance on how to answer all these types of questions throughout Chapters 1–6.

Nature
Origin
Purpose

Some examples of the type of questions NOP encourages you to ask are given below.

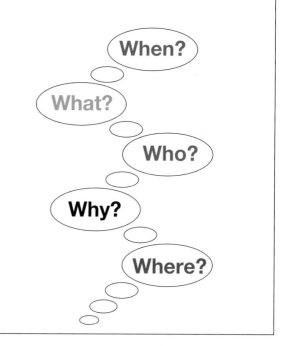

Nature

• What type of source is it?

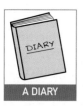

• How will this influence the utility (usefulness) of the source? For example, photographs can only capture one moment in time but can still be useful.

Origin

• Who produced the source?
• What do I know about this person or organisation?
• When was the source produced?
• Is this person or organisation likely to give a one-sided view of the event? If so, which side is not represented?

• Is it the evidence of an eyewitness? What are the advantages and disadvantages of eyewitness evidence?
• Was it written at a later date? Did the person have the benefit of hindsight?
• What are the advantages and limitations of sources that were written later?
• Under what circumstances or in what situation was the source produced? For example, some sources are written under strict government control and censorship and the person who wrote the source may not have the freedom to write what they genuinely believed.

Purpose

• Why was the source produced, written, drawn, etc?
• Is the person trying to make you support one view or one side? For example, cartoons are usually drawn to make fun of people and/or events.
• Is the source an example of propaganda? If so, what view is it trying to get across? (Be careful, propaganda sources are useful because they provide evidence of the methods used to gain support.)

Chapters 1–6 help develop these generic source skills using a variety of sources and tasks.

1 Russia before the First World War

Source A: **Cartoon showing the different groups in Russia at the beginning of the twentieth century**

Tasks

Study Source A.

1. *Each numbered arrow represents a different class or group in Russian society. Try to identify each one.*

2. *What message do you get from the cartoon about Russian society in 1900?*

Russia at the beginning of the twentieth century was a vast empire covering one-sixth of the world's surface. It was ruled by **Tsar** Nicholas II who faced a number of political, economic, social, religious and geographical problems.

This chapter will answer the following questions:

• Why was Russia so difficult to govern?
• How was Russia ruled?
• Why was the Orthodox Church so unpopular?
• Why was Nicholas II such a weak tsar?
• Why was the economy so backward?
• Why were so many people unhappy?

Source skills

In this chapter you will look at inference questions from Paper 2, but there are also questions that help you develop your understanding of the topic. Do remember that in Paper 2, you have to answer questions which focus not only on your source skills but which also examine your knowledge and understanding of a topic.

Why was Russia so difficult to govern?

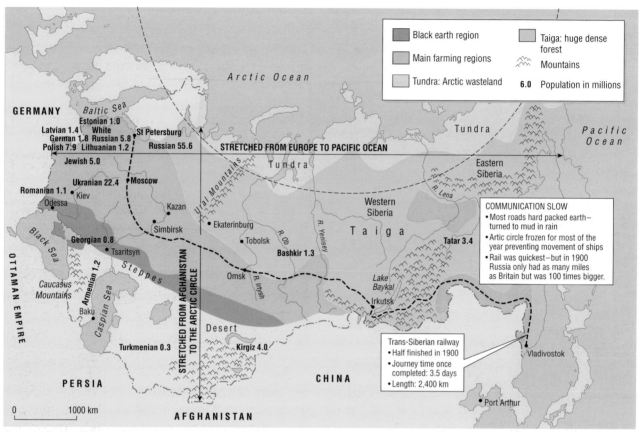

The Russian Empire in 1900

The map above shows some of the reasons why the size of the Russian Empire made it difficult to govern. It was also difficult to rule because of the many different peoples or ethnic groups in the empire. The total population of 125 million was made up of more than 20 different peoples. For six people out of every ten, Russian was a foreign language.

Many of these peoples resented being part of the empire, especially as the rulers of Russia carried out a policy of **Russification**. This meant making non-Russians speak Russian, wear Russian clothes and follow Russian customs. For example, in the area of present-day Poland, it was forbidden to teach children in Polish. Russians were often given the important jobs in non-Russian areas.

Tasks

1. *Using the map, in one sentence explain why the size of the Russian Empire made it so difficult to govern.*

2. *Why do you think the many non-Russian groups in the Russian Empire were known as the 'subject' nationalities?*

3. *What was meant by 'Russification'? Start by defining the term and then give examples of how it was carried out.*

How was Russia ruled?

Russia was an **autocracy** with all the power in the hands of the tsar. The tsar believed that he had a divine right to rule – that is, he had been chosen by God. This meant he could do whatever he liked without having to consult his people. There was no parliament to represent the people's views.

The tsar did have a council of ministers that ran the various government departments, but they could not make important decisions. There were thousands of civil servants, such as tax collectors, who carried out the day-to-day work of government. They were generally poorly paid, so this encouraged bribery and corruption.

The Russian people had little freedom. All unions of workers and strikes were forbidden, and newspapers and books were censored by the government. The tsar was determined to suppress all opposition through the *Okhrana*, his secret police. They used spies and agents to root out anyone who was against the tsar and his system of government. Such opponents could be imprisoned without trial or exiled to far-off Siberia.

Source A: Extract from a letter from Tolstoy, a Russian novelist, who wrote to Tsar Nicholas II about the discontent at the time

*A third of the whole of Russia lives under police surveillance. The army of the police, both regular and secret, is continually growing in numbers. The prisons are overcrowded with thousands of convicts and political prisoners. **Censorship** has reached its highest level since the 1840s. In all cities . . . soldiers are . . . equipped with live ammunition to be sent out against the people.*

The Orthodox Church

About 70 per cent of the population were members of the official **Orthodox Church**. The Church was very closely linked to the tsar and supported his way of ruling. It taught that the tsar was the head of the country and the Church – in other words, that he was God's chosen representative on earth.

It was unpopular because large minorities belonged to other Churches and religions, and resented the power and privileges of the Orthodox Church. For example, 9 per cent were Roman Catholic and 11 per cent Muslim. Also, the Church was very wealthy, which contrasted greatly to the poor lifestyle of the majority of Russian people.

Source B: Painting of a religious procession inside a Russian Orthodox Church *c*1990

Tasks

1. What can you learn from Source A about how Russia was ruled in 1902?

(This is an inference question. For further guidance see page 16.)

2. Why do you think Tolstoy wrote an open letter to the tsar? What was he hoping to achieve?

3. Source A gives only an extract from Tolstoy's letter. Using information from this section, add another paragraph to his letter about other reasons for discontent in Russia.

4. What can you learn from Source B about the Orthodox Church? Does it support any of the reasons about why it was unpopular?

Why was Nicholas II such a weak tsar?

The system of autocracy only worked if the tsar was strong and able to control the government and different nationalities of the vast Russian Empire. Nicholas II, who became tsar in 1894, was not a strong character. He was reluctant to become tsar, possibly because he witnessed the assassination of his grandfather, Alexander II (see biography), in 1881. When he became tsar in 1894 he said:

'What is going to happen to me? I am not prepared to be tsar. I never wanted to become one. I know nothing of the business of ruling. I have no idea of even how to talk to ministers.'

Nicholas II insisted on governing as an autocrat. He and his wife, the Tsarina Alexandra, believed that they had been chosen by God to rule and that no one had the right to challenge them. He was ignorant of the nature and extent of opposition to tsarist rule and refused to share power.

Although a devoted husband and father, he was not particularly happy. His only son and heir, Alexis, suffered from an incurable blood disease known as **haemophilia** and was likely to die young.

Source A: Extract from the diary of the tsar's sister, the Grand Duchess Olga

He had intelligence, . . . faith and courage but he was . . . ignorant about governmental matters. Nicky had been trained as a soldier. He had not been taught statesmanship and . . . was not a statesman.

Source B: Nicholas II and his family

Biography Tsar Alexander II, 1855–81

Alexander II had, in the first half of his reign, introduced a series of reforms to try to improve the Russian Empire. These included freeing the peasants from the institution of serfdom, relaxing the censorship of the press, improving conditions for soldiers in the army and making changes in education. He even brought in locally elected councils known as the *Zemstva.*

However, these changes encouraged opposition to the tsarist system of government and, during the later years of his reign, Alexander II reverted to censorship and the use of the secret police to try to suppress this opposition. In 1881, the carriage he was travelling in was blown up by a revolutionary opponent and Alexander was killed.

Tasks

1. *Does Source B support the evidence of Source A about Nicholas II? Explain your answer.*

(This is a cross-referencing question. For further guidance see page 23.)

2. *How would Nicholas have responded to Tolstoy's open letter on page 11? Write a letter of reply to Tolstoy from the tsar. Remember that he believed in the system of autocracy and the need to suppress opposition, especially after the assassination of his grandfather.*

Why was the economy so backward?

The majority of the population, 85 per cent, lived in the countryside. Russian agriculture, however, was poor. Extensive tundra, forest and desert meant only about 5 per cent of the land, mainly in the south-west, was used for farming (see map, page 10). Old-fashioned farming methods resulted in low food production and frequent famines. In most villages the land was divided into three large fields. Each household had strips in each of these fields. This scattered strip farming system encouraged **subsistence farming** using primitive hand tools.

Source A: **A photograph taken in 1892 showing starving peasants being given food during a famine**

Even though Russia was rich in oil and minerals, industrialisation did not happen until the end of the nineteenth century. This was much later than some other European countries, such as Britain and Germany, who industrialised in the late eighteenth and mid-nineteenth centuries. Considering Russia's size and resources, its manufacturing output was still very low at the beginning of the twentieth century. Its size and undeveloped system of roads and railways, together with the absence of an effective banking system, all restricted the growth of industry.

However, in the 1890s, there was a rapid growth in industry due to:

- an increase in the output of coal in the Ukraine
- an increase in the output of oil in the Caucasus
- deliberate government policy. One of the tsar's ministers, Count Sergei Witte, who was minister of finance from 1893 to 1903, set himself the huge task of modernising the Russian economy. He invited foreign experts and workers to advise on industrial planning and techniques. His reforms did stimulate industrial growth as can be seen in the table below.

Annual production (in millions of tons)				
	Coal	Pig iron	Oil	Grain*
1880	3.2	0.42	0.5	34
1890	5.9	0.89	3.9	36
1900	16.1	2.66	10.2	56
1910	26.8	2.99	9.4	74
1913	35.4	4.12	9.1	90
1916	33.8	3.72	9.7	64
(*European Russia only)				

Russia's annual industrial production from 1880 to 1913

Russia also experienced the social problems that normally go with early and rapid industrialisation. Many peasants moved to the towns and cities to work in industry. This brought problems with living and working conditions.

Tasks

1. *What can you learn from Source A about life in the Russian countryside?*

(This is an inference question. For further guidance see page 16.)

2. *Suggest two improvements to the normal farming practices that could have made it more efficient. Think about the strip farming system and the tools.*

3. *Examine the table of industrial production. Why do you think grain production increased so much in this period? (One clue is Stolypin – see page 24.)*

Why were so many people unhappy?

The Russian Empire was a land of great contrasts. As you have seen in Source A on page 9, Russian society was divided into various classes or groups. The vast majority of the people were poor peasants. At the other end of the scale, at the top, was the aristocracy.

Source A: A typical flat in St Petersburg for workers in industry in the late 1890s

Source B: A dinner party in the palace of Countess Yelisaveta Shuvalova in St Petersburg in 1900

What was life like for the wealthy?

The aristocracy made up just over one per cent of the population and yet they owned almost one-quarter of all the land. Some were extremely rich, with lavish homes in the countryside, a second home in a town or city and many servants.

Source C: Tolstoy describes the lifestyle of a Russian nobleman, Prince Dmitri Ivanovich Nechlyudov

The prince proceeded to a long dining table where three servants had polished for a whole day. The room was furnished with a huge oak sideboard and an equally large table, the legs of which were carved in the shape of a lion's paws. On this table, which was covered with a fine starched cloth with large monograms, stood a coffee pot, a silver sugar bowl, a cream jug with hot cream, and a bread basket filled with freshly baked rolls.

By 1900, Russia had a middle class whose numbers were increasing due to the development of industry. This included bankers, merchants and factory owners. Many made fortunes from government contracts and loans and had a very pleasant lifestyle; eating out at expensive restaurants and frequently going to the theatre or ballet.

Why were many peasants discontented?

The biggest, and possibly poorest group, were the peasants. They made up nearly four out of every five Russian people in 1900. For most, life was very hard. They lived in very poor conditions and survived on a staple diet of rye bread, porridge and cabbage soup. When the harvests were poor, there was starvation and disease. They had a life expectancy of less than 40 years, with many dying from typhus and diphtheria.

Many peasants felt bitter towards the nobles or aristocracy and their generally extravagant lifestyle. The nobles had kept most of the land when serfdom ended in 1861 and peasants resented having to work on nobles' estates to earn money.

A population growth of 50 per cent between 1860 and 1897 brought greater competition for land and even smaller peasant plots.

Source D: A photograph of a starving peasant family

Source E: A Russian lady who led a relief party that took food to the Volga region suffering from famine in 1892, describes what she witnessed

It was tragedy to see splendid men in the prime of their life walking about with stony faces and hollow eyes. And then there were women clothed only in wretched rags, and little children shivering in the cold wind. There were many of them who had not tasted food for days. It was agonising to hear these people pleading to us for mercy lest they die of starvation. There was no complaint, no cries, just the slow monotonous chant, broken by the sobs of worn out mothers and the cries of hungry children.

Why were many town workers unhappy?

The final and most rapidly increasing group were the new workers in industry in the towns and cities. Large numbers of peasants had flocked to the towns and cities to work in industry. Their conditions were terrible. Workers lived in overcrowded slums and ate cheap black bread, cabbage soup and wheat porridge. In industrial centres away from the cities, workers often lived in barracks next to the factory and slept in filthy, overcrowded dormitories.

They earned low wages, worked long hours and were forbidden to form trade unions to fight for better conditions. Protests or strikes were crushed, often with great brutality by the police or army.

Source F: From *The Story of My Life*, by Father Gapon written in 1905. Gapon was a priest who organised a trade union to help workers

They receive terrible wages, and generally live in overcrowded conditions. The normal working day is eleven and a half hours not including meal times. But manufacturers have received permission to use overtime. This makes the average day longer than that allowed by the law – fifteen or sixteen hours.

Tasks

1. Look again at the cartoon showing the different groups in Russian society (Source A, page 9).

   a. Do your own sketch to show these different groups.

   b. Annotate your sketch with key words to show the main features of each group.

2. Does Source D support the evidence of Sources A and B about the lifestyle of people in Russia at the beginning of the twentieth century? Explain your answer.

(This is a cross-referencing question. For further guidance see page 23.)

3. Make a copy of the following table and use the sources and information on these two pages and page 10 to complete it.

   • In the second column give a brief explanation for their discontent.

   • In the third column explain what you think the tsar should do to reduce or remove this discontent.

	Why discontented?	What tsar should do
Subject nationalities		
Peasants		
Town workers		

Examination practice

Question 1 – inference

What can you learn from Source A about the living conditions of factory workers?

(4 marks)

How to answer

This is an inference question. You are being asked to give the message of the source, to read between the lines of what is written. For example, in Source A there are several 'messages':

Question 2 – inference

What can you learn from Source B about the effects of famine on peasants in Russia?

Now have a go yourself

- Begin your answer with 'This source suggests that...'. This should help you to get a message or messages from the source.
- Avoid repeating the content.
- Look for key words in the source that might lead to inferences.
- You could tackle this by copying the source and highlighting different messages in different colours to help you identify the messages contained within, like in the example (left).

Source A

The message here could be that the apartment was overcrowded.

About fifteen of us rented one apartment. I was in a dark, windowless corner room. It was dirty and full of bedbugs and fleas. There was just enough space for two beds and I shared mine with another man. The rooms stank of the mud from the street which, itself, was made up of dirt, rubbish and sewage.

The message here could be there was a lack of ventilation.

The message here could be that workers lived in very unhealthy conditions which could cause disease.

The overall message could be that the living conditions for workers were very unpleasant.

2 Opposition to tsarist rule

Source A

From a letter, written in 1902, by novelist Count Leo Tolstoy to Tsar Nicholas II. Tolstoy is commenting on the Russian system of government

The tsarist system of government is outdated. It will be impossible to maintain this form of government except by every kind of violence, special control, exiles, executions, religious persecutions, prohibitions of books and distortion of education.

Task

What can you learn from Source A about the tsarist system in Russia in 1902?

By 1900, there were many people within Russia who opposed the tsar and it was at this time that political parties began to emerge. Opposition to tsardom was not new. There had been several revolts by the **serfs** and, in 1881, Tsar Alexander II had been assassinated by a revolutionary group called the People's Will.

What must be remembered is that although there was opposition to the tsarist system, most people did not seek to replace Nicholas II. They simply wanted reform within the existing system and there was quite a reservoir of good will towards the tsar. However, this reservoir began to run dry when he failed to introduce long-lasting reforms in the years leading up to 1917.

This chapter will answer the following questions:

- Why was there a **revolution** in 1905?
- What did the political parties believe?
- Why were the *dumas* unsuccessful?
- Why did discontent grow from 1906–14?

Source skills

This chapter reinforces some of the inference skills from the previous chapter and also gives guidance on the Paper 2 cross-reference question.

Why was there a revolution in 1905?

The Russo-Japanese War, 1904–05

Poor harvests in 1900 and 1902, along with an industrial depression, meant that, by 1904, Russia was experiencing terrible problems. Strikes, demonstrations and attacks on landlords' houses became commonplace. To add to these domestic issues, the tsar found himself facing war with Japan. Some of his advisers felt that a war would distract people's attention from domestic problems and a quick victory would end criticism and restore support and faith in tsarism.

However, the war brought military and naval disasters, and humiliation for both the tsar and Russia. Furthermore, the war produced food shortages, **inflation** and increased resentment when peasants and workers were forced to join the army. The war seemed to show how incompetent and poorly led the government was.

'Bloody Sunday', 22 January 1905

As discontent grew in Russia, around 200,000 people from St Petersburg demonstrated by marching to the tsar's Winter Palace. The march was organised by Father Gapon and the demonstrators were to give the tsar a petition (see Source A) asking for:

- a reduction in the working day
- an increase in wages
- an end to the war with Japan
- an improvement in working conditions.

The demonstrators thought that the tsar would listen to their pleas – he was, after all, their '**little father**'. Many even carried **icons** of him.

However, the tsar was not in the palace and the soldiers guarding it panicked. They eventually fired on the crowd, killing hundreds and wounding thousands. The event became known as Bloody Sunday.

Source A: An extract from the petition to the tsar, January 1905

Sire, we workers, our children, our wives and our old helpless parents have come to seek from you, truth and protection. We are impoverished and oppressed, unbearable work is imposed on us, we are despised and not recognised as human beings. We are treated as slaves and we have suffered terrible things, but we are pushed deeper and deeper into the abyss of poverty, ignorance and lack of rights. We are seeking here our last salvation.

Source B: A painting, by Vladimir Makovsky, of Bloody Sunday, 1905

Consequences of Bloody Sunday

Source C: From a letter by an American diplomat in the Russian city of Odessa. He was writing about the consequences of Bloody Sunday

Tsar Nicholas has lost absolutely the affection of the Russian people, and whatever the future may have in store for the Romanovs, Nicholas will never again be safe in the midst of his people.

Bloody Sunday seemed to be the signal for Russia to erupt into violence and, by the summer of 1905, there was chaos in both urban and rural areas. In February, the tsar's uncle, the Grand Duke Sergei was assassinated. Strikes, riots, disturbances in non-Russian parts of the empire, mutiny in the navy and an unreliable army in Moscow and St Petersburg clearly showed Nicholas and his ministers that something had to be done to restore order.

Then, in September, a general strike began and a **soviet** was established in St Petersburg. The soviet became the effective government of St Petersburg and, at last, the workers had some power. Nicholas had to act and he was persuaded by his prime minister, Witte, to publish the October Manifesto.

The October Manifesto, 1905

In order to avoid further chaos, Tsar Nicholas issued the October Manifesto. It was hoped that his promises would deal with the issues raised by the various groups within Russia during 1905.

He promised:

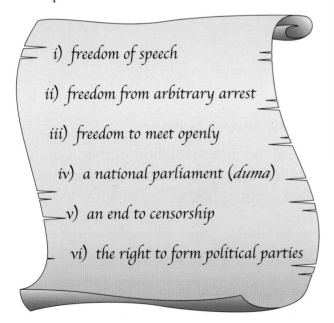

i) *freedom of speech*

ii) *freedom from arbitrary arrest*

iii) *freedom to meet openly*

iv) *a national parliament (duma)*

v) *an end to censorship*

vi) *the right to form political parties*

These promises secured the support of most of the middle classes who feared complete anarchy.

The peasants were won over when, in November, the Land Redemption Payments were stopped (these were the payments for land which peasants had been making since 1861 when serfs were freed).

The workers were not given concessions. The St Petersburg Soviet was closed down and the workers' uprising in Moscow in December was bloodily crushed by loyal troops returning from the war with Japan. Any remaining dissatisfied peasants were also harshly dealt with by the army. Bands of thugs (Black Hundreds) roamed many cities after 1905, killing hundreds of revolutionaries – the authorities did nothing to stop them.

The tsar had survived. He was fortunate because there had been no organised attempt to remove him. Each group wanted different things and, therefore, there was no real co-ordination between them. Moreover, the bulk of the army remained loyal and consequently, Nicholas was able to put down any serious threat.

Tasks

1. *What can you learn from Source A about the attitude of the demonstrators to Tsar Nicholas II?*

(Remember how to answer this type of question? For further guidance see page 16.)

2. *Look at Source B. Why do you think that Nicholas lost the support of many people after images like this were published?*

3. *Draw a concept map that shows the effects on Russia of the war with Japan.*

4. *Explain why the tsar survived the events of 1905.*

5. *Why do you think that the October Manifesto was such an important document for political development in Russia after 1905?*

What did the political parties believe?

The October Manifesto made political parties legal in Russia in 1905. Before this time they did exist, but had to meet secretly. The tsar's secret police (*Okhrana*) was used to infiltrate meetings, so this meant that some parties had members who were in jail, exile or on the run from the authorities.

Social Democratic Labour Party founded in 1898	
 Vladimir Lenin **Leon Trotsky** **Julius Martov**	The party followed the teachings of Karl Marx (see opposite for Marx's views) and believed that the workers (proletariat) would one day stage a revolution and remove the tsar. The revolution would lead to the setting up of a communist state. In 1903, the party split into two – **Mensheviks** and Bolsheviks. The Mensheviks believed that the party should have a mass membership and were prepared for slow change. The Bolsheviks believed that a small party elite should organise the revolution. Vladimir Lenin led the Bolsheviks and the Mensheviks were led by Julius Martov and Leon Trotsky.

The Socialist Revolutionaries (SRs) founded in 1901	
 **Alexander Kerensky**	The SRs, as they were called, believed in a revolution of the peasants and aimed to get rid of the tsar. They wanted to share all land among the peasants, so that it could be farmed in small peasant communities. There was a mixture of beliefs within the party – some wanted to use terror to achieve their aims and others were prepared to use constitutional methods. Terrorist activity by SR members led to the deaths of 2000 government officials in the years 1901–05. Alexander Kerensky eventually led the SRs.

Constitutional Democratic Party (Cadets) founded in 1905

Paul Milyukov

As Russia developed a middle class, the demand grew for a democratic style of government. The Cadets wanted to have a constitutional monarch and an elected parliament – as in Britain – though some were prepared to set up a republic.

The Cadets were led by Paul Milyukov.

The Octobrists founded October 1905

Alexander
Guchkov

This party was set up after the tsar issued his October Manifesto. Its followers believed that the tsar would carry out his manifesto promises of limited reform. The Octobrists' main area of support came from the middle classes.

It was led by Alexander Guchkov.

History was shaped by the struggles between different social classes…

As society changed from *feudalism* to *capitalism*, there were struggles between the aristocracy and the middle classes. The middle classes were able to take power from the aristocrats and began to exploit the workers in the new industrial world.

The workers (proletariat) would eventually rebel against their exploitation and set up a socialist state.

Eventually, the ideal state would be created – communism, where everyone was equal and people worked for the good of the commune or state.

…Marx's interpretation of history meant that a successful proletarian revolution could only occur where there was an industrial society.

The theory of Marxism

Tasks

1. *Which of the political parties might Tsar Nicholas have feared the most? Explain your answer.*

2. *Look at the theory of Marxism cartoon. Why do you think that some people in Russia were attracted to Marx's ideas?*

3. *Do you think Tsar Nicholas might have been concerned about the spread of Marxism in Russia at the end of the nineteenth century? Explain your answer.*

Why were the *dumas* unsuccessful?

Source A: **A cartoon from a Russian magazine published in 1906. The muzzled man represents the *duma* and he is flanked by two of the tsar's representatives**

The tsar had survived, but he was determined to undermine the move towards a constitutional government in Russia. Elections were held in March 1906 and the meeting of the first *duma* was held in April. However, the tsar restricted the power of the *duma* by issuing the Fundamental Laws, which prevented it from making laws, appointing ministers and controlling key areas of finance. Furthermore, Nicholas could dissolve the *duma* whenever he wanted.

Source C: **From a statement made by the tsar in 1908**

I created the duma *not to have it instruct me but to have it advise me.*

Source B: **Table of *duma* members by political grouping. 1906–14**

Parties	First *Duma*	Second *Duma*	Third *Duma*	Fourth *Duma*
PARTIES ON THE LEFT				
Social Democrats	0	65	14	14
Socialist Revolutionaries (SRs)	0	34	0	0
Trudoviks (allies of the SRs)	94	101	14	10
LIBERAL PARTIES				
Cadets	179	92	52	57
Progressives	0	0	39	47
CONSERVATIVES				
Octobrists	17	32	120	99
RIGHT-WING GROUPS	15	63	145	152
NATIONAL MINORITIES	120	130	26	21

The First *Duma*, April–July 1906

The first *duma* was radical in its approach to the problems facing Russia. The Cadets wanted **land reform** and health insurance for the workers and the Trudoviks (allies of the SRs) wanted the state to take over all land. The *duma* argued constantly with Nicholas and so he, along with Stolypin, the prime minister, decided to dissolve it. It had lasted less than two months.

After the dissolution, 200 Cadet and Trudovik deputies (members of the *duma*) withdrew to Vyborg in Finland. The deputies appealed to the people of Russia to refuse to pay taxes and defy conscription. Sporadic violence broke out across Russia and prime minister Stolypin used this as a pretext to fiercely repress any challenge to the tsar.

Source D: Statement from Nicholas dissolving the *duma*, 21 July 1906

The representatives of the nation . . . have strayed into spheres beyond their competence . . . and have been making comments upon the imperfections of the Fundamental Laws, which can only be modified by Our imperial will. In short, the representatives of the nation have undertaken illegal acts . . . We shall not permit illegal acts, and We shall impose Our imperial will on the disobedient by all the power of the State.

The Second *Duma*, February–June 1907

The new elections saw a move to the left (see Source B) – the Mensheviks won 9 per cent of the seats and the SRs won 7 per cent. The *duma* criticised the running of the army and was unwilling to work with Stolypin over land reform. Following the discovery of an alleged plot to assassinate the tsar by Social Revolutionary and Social Democrat deputies, the *duma* was dissolved.

The Third *Duma*, November 1907–June 1912

Stolypin altered the voting system for the third *duma* and this resulted in the virtual exclusion of peasant and industrial workers from the vote. There were fewer critics of the tsar and some reforms were introduced – for example, national insurance was started.

The Fourth *Duma*, November 1912–August 1914

The *duma* did not achieve much and was beset by worsening problems abroad. It was happy to go to war in 1914 and Nicholas was able to suspend it after a war budget had been passed. The *duma* did meet again in 1916 and 1917, and the Provisional Government emerged from it after the abdication of Nicholas (see page 36).

Tasks

1. *In the* dumas, *what is meant by the term* Fundamental Laws?

2. *Explain why the first* duma *lasted such a short time.*

3. *Explain why each political party might have been disappointed with the work of the* dumas *by 1912. Refer back to pages 20–21 about the different parties' aims to help you answer this question.*

4. *What can you learn from Source B about changes in the Russian political system?*

(Remember how to answer this type of question? For further guidance refer to page 16.)

Examination practice
Question 1 – cross-referencing
Does the evidence of Source C support Sources A and D about the attitude of the tsar to the *dumas*?   (6 marks)

How to answer
This question is about cross-referencing. It is the type of question that is asked for question (b) in Paper 2. In this question you will need to analyse Sources A, C and D.

To do this:
- Begin by looking at Source C and working out what it says about the tsar's attitude.
- Look at Source A and find points of agreement and/or disagreement with Source C.
- Look at Source D and find points of agreement and/or disagreement with Source C.
- Finish by making a judgement – you can do this by beginning a new paragraph. Start with the word 'Overall'.

Now answer the question, making sure that your answer is clear and direct. It must cover all three sources and, above all, there must be some judgement within the response. An examiner will be looking for such words and phrases as – 'to a degree', 'to a certain extent', 'completely', 'whereas', 'on the other hand', 'however'.

Why did discontent grow from 1906–14?

The work of Stolypin

> **Source A: A statement from Stolypin, speaking in 1906**
>
> *I must carry through effective measures of reform and at the same time I must face revolution, resist it and stop it.*

Task

1. *Look at Source A and the information about the work of Stolypin. Construct a balance sheet to show why some Russians supported Stolypin's policies and others opposed them.*

After the 1905 Revolution, Nicholas appointed Peter Stolypin as prime minister. Stolypin attempted to introduce agricultural reforms, such as encouraging peasants to buy their land and to end the practice of strip farming (see page 13). However, not all peasants were willing to change – they were rather conservative in their outlook and kept to the old system of the *mir* (**commune**). Some peasants did buy land, but this resulted in others becoming landless labourers, wandering around seeking work on the wealthier peasants' farms, or even in towns.

Stolypin improved education, encouraged industrial development and looked to create prosperity in Russia. He hoped that prosperity would prevent revolution.

However, those who openly opposed the tsar were dealt with severely. There were more than 3000 executions during Stolypin's time as prime minister – the gallows became known as 'Stolypin's necktie'. Furthermore, the policy of Russification continued, whereby Poles, Finns, Ukrainians and other nationalities lost basic **civil rights** and had their national identities challenged.

Rasputin

After 1907, Nicholas and his wife, Alexandra, came to rely on the help and guidance of a holy man named Gregory Rasputin. Rasputin had the ability to control the life-threatening illness of the tsar's son – Alexei suffered from haemophilia. Alexandra and Nicholas called Rasputin 'Our Friend' and his position and power at court grew so much that he eventually helped to choose government ministers.

Source B: A photograph of Rasputin (sitting in the centre) surrounded by courtiers

There were many aristocrats who disliked the influence of Rasputin but, equally, there were those who sought his company. Stories about his **hedonistic** lifestyle abounded, such as rumours of orgies, and there were always large numbers of women in his presence.

Rasputin was another piece of ammunition for those who did not like tsarism. These critics saw corruption and incompetence now being added to the list of problems that Russia faced.

Source C: From a statement by Rodzianko, Octobrist politician, March 1916, about the evil influence of Rasputin

I said to the Tsar – 'This cannot continue much longer. No one opens your eyes to the true role which Rasputin is playing. His presence in Your Majesty's Court undermines confidence in your Supreme Power and may have an evil effect . . .'
My report did some good – Rasputin was sent away to Tobolsk, but few days later, at the demand of the Empress, this order was cancelled.

Source D: One of the many postcards that circulated St Petersburg in 1917, showing Rasputin and Alexandra.

Tasks

2. *Look at Source B. What can you learn from Source B about the influence of Rasputin at this time?*

(Remember how to answer this type of question? For further guidance see page 16.)

3. *Study Sources B, C and D. Does Source D support the evidence of Sources B and C about the influence of Rasputin? Explain your answer.*

(Remember how to answer this type of question? For further guidance see page 23.)

Industrial unrest

Source E: Table showing strike activity in the period January 1905 to July 1914

Year	Total strikes	Political strikes
1905	13,995	6024
1906	6114	2950
1907	3573	2558
1908	892	464
1909	340	50
1910	222	8
1911	466	24
1912	2032	1300
1913	2404	1034
1914 (January–July)	3534	2401

Russia experienced an industrial boom after 1905 and with this came the growth of huge factories. As we have seen in Chapter 1 (page 15), industrial workers had poor living and working conditions. By 1912, real wages were below those of 1903 and workers were barely able to survive. One of the most important strikes occurred in 1912 at the Lena goldfields, where troops shot dead more than 200 strikers and injured several hundred.

Source F: Photograph showing some of the dead strikers at the Lena goldfields, 1912

The events at Lena heralded a new wave of strikes in urban areas across Russia and there was a general strike in St Petersburg in July 1914. However, unlike 1905, there were few disturbances in the countryside and the army could be relied on to put down any revolutionary outbursts. Furthermore, the tercentenary (300 years) celebrations of the **Romanov dynasty** in 1913 had

Source G: Photograph of townspeople and peasants in Kostroma, 1913. They were waiting to see the tsar pass by during his tercentenary tour of parts of Russia

assured Nicholas that his people still loved him. On the surface he could claim to have weathered the storm of 1905 and its aftermath, but events in the Balkans in July 1914 were to bring about his eventual downfall. The assassination of Archduke Franz Ferdinand eventually pushed Russia into war on the side of Serbia against Austria–Hungary. On 1 August 1914, Russia declared war on Germany amidst much jubilation in St Petersburg. Within three years, those same people who had cheered on the tsar were demanding the end of the Romanov dynasty.

Tasks

4. *Does Source G support the evidence of Sources E and F about support for the tsar and his government? Explain your answer.*

(Remember how to answer this type of question? For further guidance see page 23.)

5. *Copy the table below and then fill in the columns to show how opposition to the tsar was developing in the years before 1914.*

Political issues	Economic issues	Social issues

3 The impact of the First World War on Russia

Source A: An extract from the diary of Meriel Buchanan, the daughter of the British Ambassador to Russia. She describes reactions to Russian entry into the First World War

5 August 1914
The processions in the streets were carrying the Emperor's portrait with the bands playing the National Anthem. Women and girls flocked to work in the hospitals. Everywhere there is enthusiasm for the war. People are convinced that we are fighting in a just and holy war for the freedom and betterment of the world. We dream of triumph and victory. The war will be over by Christmas.

Source B: An extract from Meriel Buchanan's diary

December 1914
Grey days of biting cold, the silence of the snow hushing the bustling activity of the city to a sudden, almost disconcerting quiet. No balls, no music. The men we have danced with have lost their lives in East Prussia or were fighting in the Carpathians, the women were working in the hospitals, in field ambulances, in Red Cross trains. War! We now know the meaning of it in all its bitter and cruel truth. There are no cheering crowds, no flags carried round in procession and no bands playing the National Anthem.

Tasks

1. *What can you learn from Source A about attitudes in Russia to the war?*

2. *Does Source B support the evidence of Source A about attitudes to the war?*

Russia entered the First World War with great expectations of success. Many believed the sheer size of the Russian armies, known as the Russian steamroller, would be too strong for both Germany and Austria-Hungary. However, by the end of 1916, Russia had suffered defeat after defeat and there was growing discontent with the tsar and his government.

This chapter will answer the following questions:

• What was Russia's involvement in the First World War?
• Why did Russia suffer so many defeats?
• What effects did these defeats have?
• What were the effects of the war?

Source skills
In this chapter you will be given the opportunity to practise the inference and cross-referencing skills you have learnt in the first two chapters.

What was Russia's involvement in the First World War?

When the heir to the Austrian throne, the Archduke Franz Ferdinand, was assassinated in Serbia on 28 June 1914, Austria, supported by Germany, declared war on the Serbs. Russia was the **protector** of Serbia, so the first reason Russia joined the war in August 1914 was to help Serbia.

Secondly, Russia also went to war to support France and Britain. All three countries were members of the **Triple Entente**.

Key Terms

Protector
The rulers of Russia had influence in eastern Europe and 'looked after' the interests of nationalities in this area.

Triple Entente
An entente means an agreement between countries to co-operate with each other. The Triple Entente was formed in 1907 and although it was not a military alliance the three countries collaborated until 1917.

What were the key military events of the war on the Eastern Front, 1914–16?

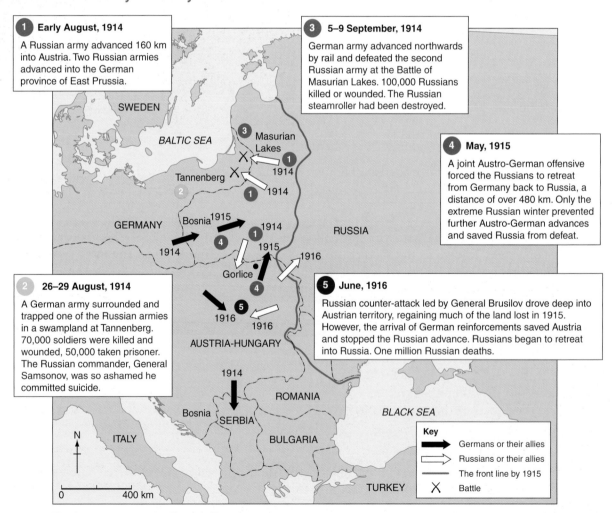

1 Early August, 1914
A Russian army advanced 160 km into Austria. Two Russian armies advanced into the German province of East Prussia.

3 5–9 September, 1914
German army advanced northwards by rail and defeated the second Russian army at the Battle of Masurian Lakes. 100,000 Russians killed or wounded. The Russian steamroller had been destroyed.

4 May, 1915
A joint Austro-German offensive forced the Russians to retreat from Germany back to Russia, a distance of over 480 km. Only the extreme Russian winter prevented further Austro-German advances and saved Russia from defeat.

2 26–29 August, 1914
A German army surrounded and trapped one of the Russian armies in a swampland at Tannenberg. 70,000 soldiers were killed and wounded, 50,000 taken prisoner. The Russian commander, General Samsonov, was so ashamed he committed suicide.

5 June, 1916
Russian counter-attack led by General Brusilov drove deep into Austrian territory, regaining much of the land lost in 1915. However, the arrival of German reinforcements saved Austria and stopped the Russian advance. Russians began to retreat into Russia. One million Russian deaths.

Key
➡ Germans or their allies
⇨ Russians or their allies
— The front line by 1915
✕ Battle

The key events on the Eastern Front, 1914–16

DATE	EVENT
August	Russians advance into Austria and Germany
26–9 August	Battle of Tannenburg
5–9 September	Battle of Masurian Lakes
	By the end of 1914 Russia had lost over 1 million men
May	Austro-German offensive
August	Nicholas takes command of the Russian armies
	By the end of 1915 Germany and Austria-Hungary had control of 13 per cent of the Russian population including 16 million people
June	Brusliov offensive
Winter	All gains from Brusliov offensive lost

Timeline of events on the Easten Front, 1914–16

Source B: The German general, von Moltke, describes the slaughter at Tannenburg

The sight of thousands of Russians driven into huge lakes and swamps was ghastly. The shrieks and cries of the dying men I will never forget. So fearful was the sight of these thousands of men with their guns, horses and ammunition, struggling in the water that, to shorten their agony, they turned the machine-guns on them. But even in spite of that, there was movement seen among them for a week after.

Source C: Germans guarding a pile of Russian corpses

Source A: A photograph showing Russian soldiers taken prisoner after the Battle of Tannenburg

Tasks

1. *What can you learn from Source B about the battle of Tannenburg?*

(Remember how to answer this type of question? For further guidance see page 16.)

2. *Does Source C support the evidence of Sources A and B about the Russian war effort? Explain your answer.*

(Remember how to answer this type of question? For further guidance see page 23.)

The impact of the First World War on Russia

Why did Russia suffer so many defeats?

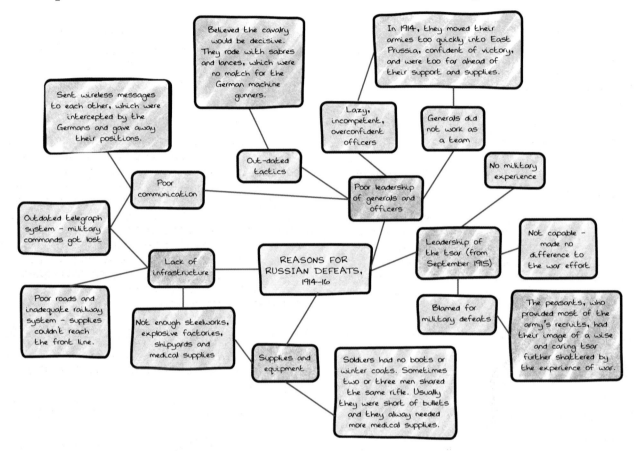

Believed the cavalry would be decisive. They rode with sabres and lances, which were no match for the German machine gunners.

In 1914, they moved their armies too quickly into East Prussia, confident of victory, and were too far ahead of their support and supplies.

Sent wireless messages to each other, which were intercepted by the Germans and gave away their positions.

Lazy, incompetent, overconfident officers

Generals did not work as a team

Out-dated tactics

No military experience

Poor communication

Poor leadership of generals and officers

Outdated telegraph system – military commands got lost

Leadership of the tsar (from September 1915)

Not capable – made no difference to the war effort

Lack of infrastructure

REASONS FOR RUSSIAN DEFEATS, 1914–16

Poor roads and inadequate railway system – supplies couldn't reach the front line.

Not enough steelworks, explosive factories, shipyards and medical supplies

Blamed for military defeats

The peasants, who provided most of the army's recruits, had their image of a wise and caring tsar further shattered by the experience of war.

Supplies and equipment

Soldiers had no boots or winter coats. Sometimes two or three men shared the same rifle. Usually they were short of bullets and they always needed more medical supplies.

Tasks

1. *Examine the concept map above, which shows the key reasons for Russia's defeats.*

- *Explain how the different reasons are linked.*
- *Rank the reasons in order of importance in the defeat of Russia.*
- *Which do you think was the most important reason for the defeats? Explain why.*

2. *You are an adviser to Nicholas II who has been sent to the Eastern Front to investigate the situation in September 1915. Write a memorandum to the tsar explaining the problems at the front and what needs to be done. Use Sources A and B and the concept map to help you.*

Source A: From a letter by the tsar to his wife in July 1916

Without metal the mills cannot supply a sufficient number of bullets and bombs. The same is true as regards the railways. The Minister of Transportation assures me that the railways are working better this year than last, but nevertheless every one complains that they are not doing as well as they might.

Source B: Written by Belaiev, a Russian general

In recent battles, a third of the men had no rifles. The poor devils had to wait patiently until their comrades fell before their eyes and they could pick up weapons. The army is drowning in its own blood.

What effects did these defeats have?

Enthusiasm for the war soon waned. Casualties, frequent defeats and poor equipment made the morale of the soldiers low. They soon lost respect for their officers who seemed unfeeling and ineffective. Many soldiers died without weapons or ammunition, and some did not even have boots to wear in the bitterly cold weather.

This discontent spread to the people of Russia. News of high casualties caused alarm in different parts of the Russian Empire. For example, in Baku, the capital of Azerbaijan, women lay on the rails to stop troop trains moving. In other areas there was violent resistance to conscription.

Source A: A police report on army morale, October 1916

The behaviour of the soldiers, especially in the units in the rear, is most provocative. They accuse the military authorities of corruption, cowardice and drunkenness, and even treason. Everywhere one meets thousands of deserters, carrying out crimes and offering violence to the civilian population.

Source B: From a report by the Chairman of the Military Commission of the *duma*

As early as the beginning of the second year of the war, desertions of soldiers at the front and on their way to the front became commonplace, and the average number of deserters reached 25 per cent. I happen to know of three cases when the train was stopped because there were no passengers on it; all, with the exception of the officer in command, had run away.

Tasks

1. *What can you learn from Source A about the effects of the war on the Russian soldiers?*

(Remember how to answer this type of question? For further guidance see page 16.)

2. *Does Source C support the evidence of Sources A and B about the effects of the war on the Russian soldiers? Explain your answer.*

(Remember how to answer this type of question? For further guidance see page 23.)

Source C: A photograph showing Russian deserters, including officers, in December 1916

DIE RUSSISCHE ARMEE LÖST SICH VÖLLIG AUF..

The impact of the First World War on Russia

What were the effects of the war?

Economic and social effects

The war had a devastating effect on the Russian economy. Inflation increased – there were seven price rises between 1913 and 1917. Less food was produced because of the shortage of labour and horses. As more peasants were called up to the armed forces, there were few men left to work on the land. Indeed, 14 million men were called up to serve in the army between 1914 and 1917. The demand for horses at the front also made it harder for peasants to cultivate their land. This, in turn, encouraged higher food prices.

Industry, too, was hit by the shortage of workers and by the lack of fuel and essential supplies. Russia did not have a transport system that could cope with the increased demands of war, as well as providing industry with the necessary raw materials. Consumer goods such as boots and cloth became scarce and expensive. There were shortages of vital coal, iron and steel. Many factories closed, making their workers unemployed.

The economic problems brought misery for many Russians. Because of the shortages, the prices were rising continually, but wages were hardly going up at all. To make matters worse, workers were being asked to work longer hours. The closure of factories led to unemployment and even greater poverty.

Wages and prices in Petrograd, 1914 and 1917 (The name St Petersburg, of German origin, was changed to Petrograd in 1914 as Russia was at war with Germany)

All these hardships were, in turn, worsened by fuel and food shortages. Even when fuel and food was available it frequently failed to reach the people in the towns and cities, due to Russia's inadequate transport system and the incompetence of the government.

Source A: From a letter by General Gurko

There is plenty of meat in Siberia but we cannot get it here because we need 300 locomotives, which we have not got. Our railways are functioning badly with all the railwaymen sent to the front at the beginning of the war. There is no one to repair the locomotives.

Source B: A photograph showing people queuing for bread in Petrograd in early 1917

What was the situation at the end of 1916?

By the end of 1916, Russia was close to defeat on the Eastern Front and there was mass discontent in the armed forces and amongst the Russian people. To make matters worse, Petrograd experienced the worst winter in living memory with temperatures falling below minus 30 degrees centigrade, at a time when there were severe food and fuel shortages.

The industrial proletariat of the capital is on the verge of despair. The smallest outbreak will lead to uncontrollable riots. Even if we assume that wages have increased by 100 per cent, the cost of living has risen by 300 per cent. The impossibility of obtaining food, the time wasted in queues outside shops, the increasing death rate due to inadequate diet and the cold and dampness as a result of the lack of coal and firewood – all these conditions have created such a situation that the mass of industrial workers are quite ready to let themselves go to the wildest excesses of a hunger riot.

Source D: From a letter written by Lenin, the leader of the Bolsheviks, who wanted to overthrow the tsarist government. It was written in December 1916

A total absence of patriotic feeling can be seen in the mood of the working masses. The high cost of living, exploitation, and the barbaric policy of the government has proved to the masses the true nature of the war. There is an increase in strikes throughout the country. Prices have gone up five to ten times compared to last year. Clothing and footwear are becoming unobtainable and you no longer talk about meat.

Tasks

1. *What can you learn from Source C about the situation in Russia at the end of 1917?*

(Remember how to answer this type of question? For further guidance see page 16).

2. *Study Source D. What evidence in the language used can you find to show that Lenin is against the government and war?*

3. *Does Source D support the evidence of Sources B and C about the situation in Russia? Explain your answer.*

(Remember how to answer this type of question? For further guidance see page 23).

Political effects

At first, the war seemed to improve the government of Russia as it encouraged the tsar to work with the *dumas*, but ultimately it seriously weakened the position of the tsar.

The tsar's decision to take over command of the war and move to the front was a serious political mistake. It meant that he left the running of the country in the hands of his wife, Alexandra, the tsarina. She refused to take advice from middle-class members of the *duma* and they became increasingly frustrated, convinced that they could do a better job.

During the war, the Russian people grew to hate anything German. They even changed the name of their capital city from the German St Petersburg to Petrograd. Alexandra was German and there were rumours that she was a German spy trying to sabotage the Russian war effort.

Rasputin was the only person Alexandra was prepared to listen to. Indeed, he seemed to be in charge of the government. The tsarina frequently dismissed any capable ministers from the *duma* on Rasputin's advice and replaced them with his own friends, who were totally incompetent. There were so many changes of ministers that nobody was organising food, fuel and other supplies to the cities properly. The railway system fell into chaos and trainloads of food were left rotting in the sidings.

As news from the war got worse and the situation in the cities got more desperate, support for the tsar and his wife began to decrease among the middle and upper classes. They blamed the tsar for leaving the country under the control of a German woman influenced by a mad monk.

Source E: Extract from a secret police report, early 1916

The filthy gossip about the Tsar's family has now become the property of the street. We must also note together with this feeling of extreme disrespect for the person of Her Majesty the Empress Alexandra the widespread feeling against her as a 'German'. Her Majesty is regarded, even in intellectual circles, as the inspirer and leader of the campaign for a separate peace with Germany.

Source F: Rasputin at a tea party

The death of Rasputin

Members of the royal family begged Alexandra to dismiss Rasputin. When she refused, some, led by Prince Yusupov, in desperation, decided to assassinate him. One evening in December 1916, Rasputin was invited to Yusopov's mansion for a social evening. During the course of the evening he ate cakes laced with enough cyanide to kill several men. He collapsed but then stood up and ran into the courtyard. There he was shot twice. His hands were bound behind him and his body thrown into the icy river where he drowned.

Rasputin's death has aroused much controversy. A recent television programme, in which an ex Scotland Yard detective visited Russia and investigated all the evidence, suggested that the British secret service may have been involved. The Russian assassin, Prince Yusupov, wrote that he shot Rasputin twice. Yet the forensic evidence on Rasputin's body, showed three bullet wounds. Did a member of the British secret service, fire the third bullet?

Tasks

4. *What can you learn from Source E (page 33) about attitudes towards the tsarina?*

(Remember how to answer this type of question? For further guidance see page 16.)

5. *Study Source F. What image does it give of Rasputin?*

6. *Read the box on Rasputin's death.*

   a. *Devise an eye-catching headline in a Russian newspaper announcing Rasputin's death.*

   b. *Using evidence from Chapter 2 (pages 24–5) and this page, write an obituary for Rasputin for the same newspaper.*

7. *Look at the circles below. This is known as a Venn diagram. They are used to show how factors can overlap with each other – how one factor can influence another.*

   - *Sketch your own Venn diagram like the one below.*

   - *Use your diagram to show the overlap between the military, political, economic/social effects. One example has been done for you, showing the leadership of Rasputin and the tsarina.*

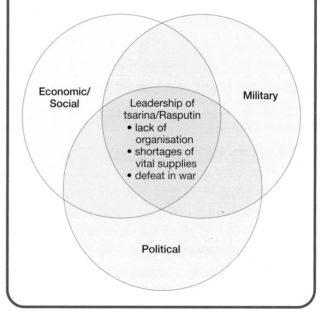

Russia in 1917

4

Source A	
From a letter written in February 1917 by a 14-year-old boy describing the situation in Petrograd	Terrible things are happening in Petrograd. It has become a real battlefield. Five regiments of the army have joined the revolt. Gunfire never ceases in our part of the city. The officers cannot go into the streets, because the crowd disarms them and even kills them … Worst of all, the soldiers have got hold of vodka and are drunk.

Task

What can you learn from Source A about the situation in Petrograd in 1917?

By the beginning of January 1917, the position in Russia was becoming chaotic. Defeats in the war, food shortages and lack of reform had meant that support for the tsar had been severely eroded. In early March, Nicholas abdicated and a Provisional Government was set up to run Russia until elections could be held. After the elections, a permanent government would be established. The Provisional Government had some successes initially but, by the autumn of 1917, it was challenged by the Bolsheviks and, in October, the Bolsheviks seized power.

This chapter will answer the following questions:

- Why was there a revolution in Russia in February 1917?
- What were the successes and failures of the Provisional Government?

Source skills
The chapter reinforces some of the inference and cross-referencing skills from the previous chapters. It also looks at the utility (usefulness) question (c) on Paper 2.

Why was there a revolution in Russia in February 1917?

Source B: From a letter written by Grand Duke Michael to the tsar in January 1917. He was describing the problems facing Russia at that time

The unrest continues to grow. Those who defend the idea that Russia cannot exist without a tsar are losing the ground under their feet, since the facts of disorganisation and lawlessness are obvious. A situation like this cannot last long. It is impossible to rule the country without paying attention to the voice of the people and without meeting their needs.

As you have learnt in Chapter 3, the First World War placed a tremendous strain on the tsarist system and, by early 1917, it seemed as if the country was on the verge of collapse. It had been hoped that the murder of Rasputin in December 1916 would help to bring some stability to the running of the country – it did not. The winter weather was especially severe in December and January and this meant that food supplies to cities and towns were affected. Prices rose and rationing only led to further discontent. In Petrograd, there were strikes and people began to demand food.

Source C: From an *Okhrana* report in January 1917 describing the mood in Petrograd

The proletariat of the capital is on the verge of despair. Time wasted in queues hoping for food to arrive, the increasing death rate due to inadequate diet, cold and dampness as a result of lack of coal and firewood have created a situation whereby the mass of industrial workers are quite ready to let themselves go to the wildest excesses of a hunger riot ... the masses led by the more advanced and already revolutionary minded elements, assume an openly hostile attitude towards the government and protest with all the means at their disposal against the continuation of the war.

Source D: Table showing prices in Petrograd, 1914 and 1916 (figures are in roubles).

Item	1914	1916
Rent for part of a room	2–3 per month	8–12 per month
Dinner in a tea room	0.15–0.20	1 or 2
Tea in a tea room	0.07	0.35
A pair of boots	5–6	20–30
Shirt	0.75–0.90	2.50–3.00

Strikes became an everyday occurrence in Petrograd in early 1917 and this resulted in huge numbers of people on the streets. The situation worsened when the soldiers **garrisoned** in Petrograd **mutinied** and began to take sides with the demonstrators. For Nicholas, this was disastrous – a loyal army had saved him in 1905 (see page 19) – now his final pillar of support started to crumble. The *duma* took control and set up a **Provisional Committee** on 12 March to take over the government. When Nicholas tried to return to Petrograd to assume the reins of government, he found his way blocked. At this, he decided to **abdicate**. The Romanov dynasty was now at a close and had reached the point where it ended itself. The abdication of Nicholas and the emergence of the Provisional Government out of the *duma* is called the February Revolution. The abdication took place in a railway carriage 320 km from Petrograd (see Source E).

Source E: The abdication of Nicholas II, March 1917. Nicholas is seated

Tasks

1. Study Sources B and D. What can you learn about the situation in Petrograd at the beginning of 1917?

(Remember how to answer this type of question? For further guidance see page 16.)

2. Study Sources A (on page 35), B and C. Does Source C support the evidence of Sources A and B about the situation in Petrograd in 1917? Explain your answer.

(Remember how to answer this type of question? For further guidance see page 23.)

3. In what ways does Source D help you to understand why many Russians had come to oppose the war by 1917?

4. What can you learn about the abdication of Nicholas II from Source E?

5. Design a newspaper headline and write an article to accompany it, explaining why Tsar Nicholas II abdicated.

Examination practice

Question (c) on Paper 2 asks you to decide the utility (usefulness) of two sources. This is worth eight marks. The best answers explain the utility and limitations of each source through:

- The content – what the sources show or say, what views they have about the event. This can get you to the top of Level 2, which is six marks
- NOP – the nature, origin and purpose of each source. You must analyse these aspects to reach Level 3, which is eight marks

Question 1 – utility

How useful are Sources B and C (page 36) as evidence of the mood of people in Petrograd in January 1917?   (8 marks)

How to answer

First, let us concentrate on content. Then we will look at NOP (page 38) and content. For each source you should think about the following questions:

1 What is useful about the content of the source?
   - What does it mention?
   - What view does it give about the feelings of people? Do you think this was a typical view of the time?

2 Are there any limitations to the content? For example:
   - Does it give a very limited and/or one-sided view?
   - What does it *not* tell us about the mood in Petrograd?

Examination practice

Nature, origin and purpose

In order to reach higher level marks for the utility question you have to explain the value (usefulness) and limitations of the NOP of each source. This is found in the provenance of the source – the information given above or below it. A good tip is to highlight or underline key words in the provenance.

NOP means:

N Nature of the source
What type of source is it? A speech, a photograph, a cartoon, a letter, an extract from a diary? How will the type of the source affect its utility? For example, a private letter is often very useful because the person who wrote it generally gives their honest views.

O Origin of the source
Who wrote or produced the source? Are their views worth knowing? Are they giving a one-sided view? When was it produced? It could be an eyewitness account. What are the advantages and disadvantages of eyewitness accounts?

P Purpose of the source
Why was the source produced? For example, the purpose of adverts is to make you buy the products; people usually make speeches to get your support. How will this affect the utility of the source? A speech might play on a crowd's feelings by exaggerating the issue and distorting the picture.

Now let us apply this to Source B (page 36).

Question 2 – utility

How useful is Source B as evidence of the situation in Russia in 1917?

• First look at how useful the source is in its NOP.

Example

Source B is useful because it is a letter (nature) written by a close relative of the tsar in 1917 (origin) and is inferring that if there is no change in the system of governing then there will be serious problems in the future (purpose). It is useful because the writer explains how bad the situation is – normally people were unwilling to speak the truth to the tsar. Furthermore, it is a private letter and here one would expect the truth to be told.

• Then look at whether the source has any limitations in its NOP.

Example

Source B is of limited use because it is an extract from a letter (nature) by an individual who was opposed to change. Therefore it might deliberately exaggerate (purpose) in order to push the tsar into action to save the system and thus the letter writer's own position in Russia.

Question 3 – utility
Now have a go yourself

How useful is Source F as evidence of food shortages in Russia in 1917?

Source F: Photograph of a bread queue in Petrograd in 1917

Make a copy of the following grid and use it to plan your answer.

	Usefulness	Limitations
Contents		
What does the source tell you?		
What view does the source give?		
According to your knowledge of this topic do you think this is a typical/popular view?		
Is the view limited?		
NOP		
Nature		
Origin		
Purpose		

Remember:

• content only Level 2 – up to six marks
• content and NOP to reach Level 3 – seven or eight marks.

The utility of two sources

In the examination you will be asked to explain the utility of two sources.

Source G: A letter from the tsarina to Nicholas, 26 February 1917

This is a hooligan movement, young people run about and shout that there is no bread, simply to create excitement, along with workers who prevent others from working. If the weather were very cold they would all probably stay at home. But all this will pass and become calm, if only the duma will behave itself.

Source H: From the diary of Sybil Grey, an English woman living in Petrograd. The entry was dated 23 February 1917

Today I saw a poor woman enter a bread shop and ask for bread. She was told there was none. On leaving the shop, seeing some bread in the window, she broke the glass and took the bread. A general, passing in his motor car, stopped and told her off. A crowd collected round them and smashed his car.

Question 4 – utility

How useful are Sources G and H as evidence of unrest in Russia in 1917?

(8 marks)

How to answer

For each source in turn:

• outline the value of its contents
• outline the value of its NOP
• outline the limitations of its contents
• outline the limitations of its NOP.

In your conclusion give a final judgement that compares the value of the two sources.

Here is a planning grid to help you:

Source G is useful because (contents) . . .

Moreover, Source G is also useful because of (NOP) . . .

Source G is of limited use because (contents) . . .

Source G is also of limited use because (NOP) . . .

Source H is useful because (contents) . . .

Furthermore, Source H is also useful because of (NOP) . . .

Source H is of limited use because (contents) . . .

Source G is also of limited use because (NOP) . . .

Overall Source G and H are useful because they . . .

Moreover, Source G is more useful because . . .

What were the successes and failures of the Provisional Government?

Source A: Photograph of soldiers and demonstrators in Petrograd, 10 March 1917. The slogan on the banner reads 'Down with the monarchy'

Task

1. Study Source A. What can you learn about the extent of unrest in Petrograd from this source?

(Remember how to answer this type of question? For further guidance see page 16.)

The end of tsarism was unplanned and took people by surprise. The Provisional Government was set up in March 1917 and it promised to bring reforms to Russia. There would also be elections for a new **Constituent Assembly** as soon as possible. The Provisional Government consisted of a cabinet of minsters (see Source B). The Prime Minister was Prince Lvov, a wealthy aristocratic landowner, and other leading figures included:

- Milyukov – Foreign Minister – leader of the Cadets
- Guchkov – War Minister – leader of the Octobrists
- Kerensky – Minister of Justice – Social Revolutionary.

The remaining ministers were chosen from the Octobrist and Cadet parties. Thus, the new government was composed of middle-class politicians who wanted to draw up a constitution and establish a democratic government.

Source B: Collage of photographs of the ministers of the Provisional Government, March 1917

The Provisional Government's problems

Source C: **From the book *The Catastrophe* by Alexander Kerensky, 1927. Here Kerensky was describing the problems of the Provisional Government**

*The new government inherited nothing from tsardom but a terrible war, an acute food shortage, a paralysed transportation system, an empty treasury, and a population in a state of furious discontent and **anarchic** disintegration.*

The Provisional Government faced a number of problems as soon as it was formed (as outlined by Kerensky in Source C):

- It was not a truly elected body and did not represent the people of Russia
- There were defeats in the war
- Soldiers were deserting
- Peasants were looting the property of the landlords
- Soldiers and workers were setting up soviets in towns and cities
- People wanted an end to food shortages
- Some of the national minorities, for example, Poles and Finns, were hoping that there might even be a chance of independence in the near future.

Perhaps the most serious issue facing the Provisional Government was the formation of the Petrograd Soviet of Workers' and Soldiers' Deputies. The soviet was an elected body of about 3,000 people and contained many revolutionaries, especially Social Revolutionaries and Mensheviks (see pages 20–21). It issued Soviet Order Number One (see Source D below) and it was this which took away much of the authority of the new government.

Source D: **Soviet Order Number One, 14 March 1917**

The Soviet of Workers' and Soldiers' Deputies has resolved:

In all its political actions, troop units are subordinate to the Soviet.

All types of arms must be kept under the control of the company and battalion committees and in no case turned over to officers, even at their demand.

The orders of the State Duma shall be executed only in such cases as do not conflict with the orders of the Soviet of Workers' and Soldiers' Deputies.

In spite of Soviet Order Number One, the Provisional Government decided to continue the war. There were even some Bolsheviks – Stalin and Kamenev – who felt that the war should not be stopped. However, the decision to continue the war was fatal for the Provisional Government because further defeats served only to create unpopularity. Defeats led to desertions and when soldiers returned home they took part in seizing land from the nobility – thus adding to the chaos.

To add to the misery of the Provisional Government, Germany sent exiled revolutionaries back to Russia in the hope that they would foment rebellion. Among these was Lenin, the Bolshevik leader, who arrived in Petrograd in April 1917. Lenin called for the overthrow of the Provisional Government.

Tasks

2. *Look at all of the problems that faced the Provisional Government. Copy the table below, placing the problems in the appropriate column and number them in what you think is their order of importance.*

Political problems	Economic problems	Military problems

3. *Study Source D. Explain why Soviet Order Number One was so important in undermining the Provisional Government.*

(Remember how to answer this type of question? For further guidance see page 16).

The Provisional Government's reforms

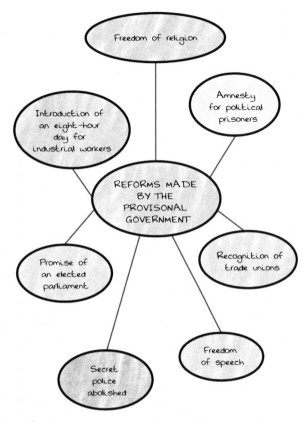

The reforms made by the Provisional Government

Diagram labels:

- Freedom of religion
- Amnesty for political prisoners
- Introduction of an eight-hour day for industrial workers
- REFORMS MADE BY THE PROVISONAL GOVERNMENT
- Recognition of trade unions
- Promise of an elected parliament
- Secret police abolished
- Freedom of speech

However, the decision to continue the war was fatal for the Provisional Government. In May, Guchkov and Milyukov were forced to resign, because they wanted to fight the war beyond the removal of German troops from Russian soil. In the following month, the Russian army suffered heavy casualties in a new offensive against the Germans. Nevertheless, the first **All-Russian Congress of Soviets** meeting in June 1917 gave a vote of confidence in the Provisional Government. (Only 105 out of 822 representatives in the Congress were Bolsheviks.)

The July Days

Despite the vote of confidence, by July, the Provisional Government was still experiencing problems. The war was not going well and the growing power of the soviets and strength of opposition were key concerns. The Austrian Front was disintegrating and this caused many soldiers to flood back to Russia. For three days, there was chaos in Petrograd when the soldiers and some Bolsheviks tried to overthrow the Provisional Government. The riots and disorder were only restored when Kerensky, the Minister of War, was able to move loyal troops to quash the rebels (see Source E). When Lenin fled the country and other

Despite its many problems, the Provisional Government did make some reforms during the early weeks of its ministry. Each reform tried to address problems which had either not been solved after the 1905 Revolution, or had been created by the tsar and his ministers in an effort to keep a tight control over the Russian people. The reforms were quite wide-ranging and it was hoped that the workers and the middle classes would be satisfied by them.

Source E: Demonstrators in Petrograd being fired upon by police during the July Days, 1917

leading Bolsheviks were arrested or went into hiding, it appeared as if their chance to seize power had gone and that the party was in decline.

Consequences of the July Days

- A new government was set up with Kerensky as prime minister. He accused the Bolsheviks of being German spies, because he knew that Lenin's return to Russia had been financed by Germany. Moreover, much of the Bolsheviks' revolutionary activity since April had been backed by German money.
- The Bolsheviks were denounced as traitors – their newspaper, *Pravda,* was closed down, Lenin fled the country and Kamenev was arrested.

However, the Bolsheviks were not finished. Lenin directed them from Finland and they were able to continue to function and maintain their high profile. Lenin altered his views about the peasants and their role in any revolution. He accepted the land seizures and encouraged even more, thus winning support in the countryside. The slogan 'land to the peasants' was taken up by the Bolsheviks.

Furthermore, Lenin knew that the Russian army could be swayed towards the Bolshevik anti-war policy – the majority of soldiers were really 'peasants in uniform'. The new slogan of 'Peace, Land and Bread' began to attract more and more followers during these critical times.

Source F: A cartoon from *Petrogradskaia Gazeta,* 7 July 1917. The *Gazeta* was a pro-government newspaper. The caption at the top reads 'A high post for the leaders of the rebellion'. The caption below reads 'Lenin wants a high post? …Well? A position is ready for him!!!'

Tasks

4. *Study Source F. What can you learn from this source about the attitude of some of the Petrograd press to Lenin and the Bolsheviks?*

(Remember how to answer this type of question? For further guidance see page 16.)

5. *How useful is Source C (page 41) in helping you to understand why the July Days happened?*

(Remember how to answer this type of question? For further guidance see pages 37–39.)

Kornilov Revolt

After the July Days, Alexander Kerensky was appointed the new prime minister. It seemed as if the Provisional Government was in control – it was not. This was shown in the Kornilov Revolt.

In September 1917, General Kornilov, the Supreme Commander-in-Chief of the armed forces threatened to seize power in Petrograd. Kornilov did not agree with the Petrograd Soviet's wish to end the war and he sought to set up a **military dictatorship**. As Kornilov and his forces approached Petrograd, Kerensky allowed the Bolshevik **Red Guards** to arm and was happy to see the Bolsheviks persuade many of Kornilov's troops to desert. Railway workers prevented Kornilov's troops from approaching Petrograd and printers stopped publication of newspapers that supported the *coup d'etat*. The *coup* failed.

Following this, Kerensky's government looked rather weak (see Source G) and the Bolsheviks, who had secured control of the Petrograd and Moscow Soviets (Trotsky was now chairman of the Petrograd Soviet), were in the ascendancy. Lenin, in exile in Finland, began to make plans not only for his return to Petrograd but also for the Bolshevik seizure of power.

The details and events of the Bolshevik Revolution are to be found in the next chapter.

Source G: From *The Russian Revolution* by D. Footman, 1962

*After the Kornilov Revolt, Kerensky and his cabinet were still in power. But there had been a striking change in the mood throughout the country. The Bolsheviks could now claim to have been the leaders in the 'victory over the **counter-revolution**' and their power and influence increased rapidly.*

All the problems that the Provisional Government had faced in February had not gone away and by October it retained little authority. Lenin's promises of 'Peace, Bread, Land', were proving more attractive than the seeming inaction of Kerensky. It is ironic that when Kerensky did act – setting the date of the elections for the Constituent Assembly – it pushed Lenin to decide on a takeover.

Tasks

6. Explain the importance of the Kornilov Revolt for the Bolsheviks.

7. Look back over this chapter and complete the following task:

Why was the Provisional Government in a precarious position by October 1917?

Answer by constructing a diagram as below, with the most important reasons at the top and moving in a clockwise direction.

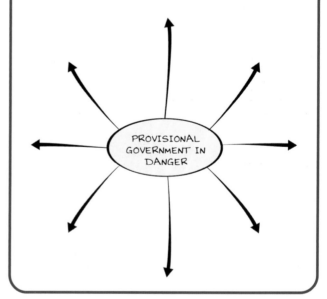

5 The nature of the Bolshevik takeover

Source A

P. Sorokin, a Socialist Revolutionary describing the Bolshevik attack on the Provisional Government on 7 November 1917

... I learned that the Bolsheviks had brought up the warship Aurora and had opened fire on the Winter Palace, demanding the surrender of the members of the Provisional Government still barricaded there ...There was a regiment of women and young military trainees bravely resisting an overwhelming force of Bolshevik troops ... Poor women, poor lads, their situation was desperate, for we knew the wild sailors would tear them to pieces.

Task

What can you learn from Source A about the Bolshevik attack on the Provisional Government in 1917?

The Bolshevik Party seized power in October 1917 with very little opposition. The Provisional Government was removed with ease and Lenin established a government based on the ideas of Karl Marx. Although the Bolshevik Party had been quite insignificant before 1905, and after the October Manifesto, the leading Bolsheviks were determined and dedicated, never losing sight of their goal. The First World War created the opportunity for their success.

This chapter will answer the following questions:

- How did the Bolshevik Party strengthen?
- What was the role of Lenin?
- What was the role of Trotsky?
- What were the main events of the Bolshevik Revolution?
- Why were the Bolsheviks successful?

Source skills

The chapter also gives advice on how to answer the synthesis question (d) on Paper 2.

How did the Bolshevik Party strengthen?

Lenin and a group of his revolutionary colleagues

Biography Vladimir Illich Ulyanov (assumed name Lenin) 1870–1924.

Key events to 1917:

1870 Born Vladimir Illich Ulyanov

1887 Elder brother, Alexander, hanged as a conspirator in the attempted assassination of Tsar Alexander III

1897 Exiled to Siberia – adopted the name Lenin

1898 Married Nadezhda Krupskaya

1902 Wrote 'What is to be done?' in which he put forward the central role of dedicated party members in any revolution

1903 Led the Bolsheviks in the Social Democrat Party split

1905 Returned to Russia – played no part in the Revolution

1906 Exiled for much of the next eleven years

1912 Secured control of the Central Committee (the body responsible for making policies)

1917 Returned to Russia

1917 Led Bolshevik Revolution and overthrew the Provisional Government

The Bolsheviks emerged from the All-Russian Social Democratic Party, which had been formed in 1898 and based its ideas on the writings of Karl Marx (see page 21).

In 1903, at the second congress of the party, there was fierce debate between those who wished to have a broad-based membership and those who wanted a narrow, more professional group of activists. The latter, led by Lenin, claimed to have won the arguments and they became known as the Bolsheviks (majority). The others, led by Martov, were known as the Mensheviks (minority).

By 1912, the two groups were essentially separate parties and each had developed different policies and interpretations of Marxism.

The Bolsheviks were not the largest revolutionary party and they played little part in the 1905 Revolution. Lenin spent little time in Russia in the years 1904–17 and he had to send his instructions to the Bolsheviks from his places of exile. Lenin persuaded the Bolsheviks not to take part in the elections for the *duma* in 1906, because they did not believe that Tsar Nicholas would keep to his promises.

After 1906, Lenin fought desperately to keep the party and spirit of revolution alive. Party funds were built up by a series of robberies – called 'expropriations' – and hundreds took place each year before 1914.

It has been estimated that before the First World War, the number of Bolsheviks never exceeded 10,000. Moreover, the *Okhrana* (secret police) did not think that the Bolsheviks were a strong threat to tsarism at this time.

The First World War

When war broke out in 1914, Lenin was in Austria. He was arrested, but allowed to travel to Zurich in neutral Switzerland. He was utterly opposed to the war, but found that there were many Bolsheviks who supported it. Moreover, there were many **socialists** in Europe who also supported the war and this seemed to show that Lenin was out of step with current thinking.

Source A: From the writings of Charles Rappaport, a Russo-French socialist in 1914. He was discussing Lenin's work

We recognised Lenin's achievements. He is a man of iron will and an incomparable organiser of groups. But Lenin regards only himself as a Socialist. Whoever opposes him is forever condemned by him . . . War is declared on anyone who differs with him . . .

Source B: From *Endurance and Endeavour* by J.N. Eastwood, a book about Lenin and the Russian Revolution, published in 1973. He was writing about Lenin's character

*He brought to the Socialists a rare hardness in discussion . . . He would not compromise, would not admit that his **ideological** enemies might be partly correct. His friends were only his friends so long as their ideas coincided.*

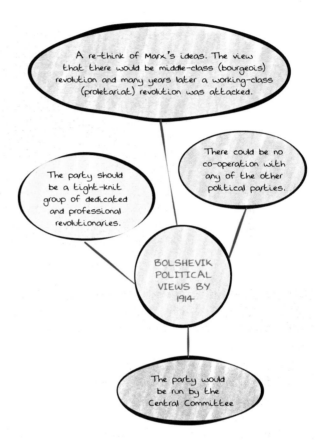

Political views of the Bolsheviks by 1914

Tasks

1. Study Sources A and B.

What can you learn about Lenin's character from these two sources?

(Remember how to answer this type of question? For further guidance see page 16.)

2. *Study the concept map above. Can you suggest reasons why Lenin was changing the views and organisation of the Bolsheviks?*

What was the role of Lenin?

After the February Revolution, Lenin was desperate to return to Russia. He was keen that his supporters at home put forward the message that the Bolsheviks wanted peace and an end to the chaos in Russia. The Germans decided to help Lenin return from exile in Switzerland, in the hope that he would overthrow the new government in Russia. The Germans thought that if Russia pulled out of the war, then more troops could be moved to the Western Front to fight Britain and France.

Lenin was put in a sealed train and sent across Germany and Sweden. He arrived in Petrograd at the Finland Station on 3 April 1917. The price to pay for this method of arrival was the accusation that he was a German spy, in the pay of the enemy. Lenin was unconcerned. He had returned and, moreover, the money from the Germans would help finance his revolution.

> **Source A: From the *Memoirs of Lenin* written by Krupskaya (Lenin's wife) published in 1970. Here she was describing Lenin's arrival at the Finland Station**
>
> *The Petrograd masses, workers, soldiers and sailors came to meet their leader . . . There was a sea of people all around. Red banners, a guard of honour of sailors, searchlights from the fortress of Peter and Paul decorated the road . . . armoured cars, a chain of working men and women guarded the road.*

The April Theses

Lenin made it clear to his followers that he would not support the Provisional Government. He wanted a workers' revolution and his plans were set out the day after his return, in what became known as the April Theses.

A 1930s painting of Lenin's arrival at the Finland station in 1917

April Theses

i) The war with Germany had to end.

ii) Power had to pass from the middle classes to the working classes.

iii) All land had to be given to the peasants.

iv) The police, army and bureaucracy should be abolished.

v) The capitalist system had to be overthrown by the workers – banks, factories and transport should be nationalised.

vi) The Bolsheviks should take control of the soviets in order to achieve their aims. The slogan 'All power to the soviets' became the watchword.

The Bolsheviks did grow in popularity and, by June 1917, there were more than 40 newspapers that spread Lenin's views and ideas across Russia. The Bolsheviks even had their own 'Red Guard' – by July, there were about 10,000 armed workers in Petrograd itself.

Tasks

1. *How useful is Source A in helping you to understand the attraction of Lenin in 1917?*

(Remember how to answer this type of question? For further guidance see pages 37–39.)

2. *Construct a table like the one below and explain why each group would support or oppose the April Theses.*

APRIL THESES	SUPPORT	OPPOSE
Workers		
Middle Classes		
Peasants		
Soldiers		

The decision to seize power

The July Days caused problems for the Bolsheviks, because Lenin was exiled again. However, following the Kornilov Revolt (see page 44), Lenin began to contemplate his return to Russia in order to begin his long-awaited revolution. In his words, the Provisional Government was 'ripe for plucking'. Because of the Kornilov Revolt, the Bolsheviks were able to say that they were the true defenders of Petrograd.

The All-Russian Congress of Soviets was due to meet in late October and it was possible that the Bolsheviks would not have a majority of representatives in it. If, however, the Bolsheviks overthrew the Provisional Government before this, they could present their new authority as a *fait accompli,* which the Congress would find difficult to reject.

Furthermore, Lenin was also aware that the Bolsheviks were unlikely to win a majority of seats in the Constituent Assembly – but if they were in power before the elections, then the results could be ignored if they were unfavourable.

Lenin was calling for a revolution, but he still remained in Finland, despite the fact that the Provisional Government had released all political prisoners who had been arrested in July. He finally returned on about 7 October and then went into hiding. On 10 October, the Bolshevik Central Committee agreed in principle on an uprising, but two influential leaders – Kamenev and Zinoviev – voiced strong objections. These two published their objections in a newspaper, alerting Kerensky to the imminent Bolshevik threat. Lenin was furious.

On 23 October, Kerensky tried to remove the Bolshevik threat – he closed down the Bolshevik papers (*Pravda* and *Izvestiya*) and attempts were made to round up leading Bolsheviks. The Bolsheviks were forced into action and Lenin ordered the revolution to begin before Kerensky could capture them. Thus, ironically, Kerensky had decided the exact timing of the revolution.

Source B: Membership of the Bolshevik Party, 1917		
February: 24,000	April: 100,000	October: 340,000 (60,000 in Petrograd)

Tasks

3. *Study Source B. What can you learn about the growth of the Bolshevik Party in 1917?*

(Remember how to answer this type of question? For further guidance see page 16.)

4. *Draw a concept map to show why Lenin felt that the Bolsheviks should attempt a revolution in October 1917.*

5. *Consider the events of 1917. Construct a balance sheet using the headings below to weigh up whether Lenin was the main architect of the revolution or whether other factors were more important.*

Lenin's role	Other factors

The nature of the Bolshevik takeover

What was the role of Trotsky?

Biography Leon Trotsky 1879–1940

1879 Born Lev Davidovich Bronstein
1897 Involved in organising the South Russian Workers' Union
1898 Arrested and spent four years in exile in Siberia
1902 Escaped and fled to London, assuming the name Trotsky
1902 Joined the Social Democratic (SD) Party. Met and worked with leading SD members
1903 Followed Martov and became a Menshevik
1905 Returned to St Petersburg and was eventually elected Chairman of the Soviet
1905 Arrested and imprisoned
1906 Exiled to Siberia but escaped after two years
1908 Worked in Vienna publishing the journal *Pravda*
1914 Moved to Zurich, and then Paris, where he denounced the war and encouraged workers not to fight
1916 Deported to Spain and then went to the USA
1917 Returned to Russia in May
1917 Chairman of Petrograd Soviet in September and member of **Military Revolutionary Committee (MRC)**
1917 **Commissar** for Foreign Affairs
1918 Commissar for War
1929 Expelled from the Communist Party
1940 Assassinated on the orders of Stalin in Mexico City

Military Revolutionary Committee (MRC)
A body originally set up by Social Revolutionaries and the Social Democrats to defend against Germany and counter-revolution.

> Key Term

Source A: From *Memoirs of a Revolutionary* by Victor Serge. Serge was a Bolshevik, writing in 1945 about Trotsky's skills as a leader

*I first saw Trotsky at a packed meeting of the Petrograd Soviet. He was all tension and energy. He outshone Lenin through his **oratorical** talent, his organising ability, first with the army and then with the railways, and by his brilliant gift as a student of political theory . . .*

Task

1. *Study Source A (on page 47) and Source A (above). In what ways were the characters of Trotsky and Lenin similar?*

As you can see from his biographical details, Trotsky was in exile at the time of the February Revolution. On his return to Russia in May 1917, he was concerned that many Mensheviks were supporting the Provisional Government. He was arrested in July as a result of his revolutionary activities and the following month he became an official Bolshevik Party member.

When the Bolsheviks secured control of the Petrograd Soviet, Trotsky was elected as its leader and this became the key to his success.

In October, he became the dominant member of the three-man Military Revolutionary Committee (MRC) of the Soviet. This provided a useful screen for his secret preparations. The MRC – in theory – controlled 20,000 Red Guards, 60,000 Baltic sailors and the 150,000 soldiers of the Petrograd garrison.

From his office in the Smolny Institute, a building formerly used as a girls' school, Trotsky made his plans for the seizure of the key buildings of the Provisional Government.

In October, the Bolsheviks began to reduce their massive demonstrations and street skirmishes, because the crowds were not always easy to control. When they started preparing for the revolution, they began to rely more on small, disciplined units of soldiers and workers. The Bolsheviks, under the leadership of Trotsky, prepared for their overthrow of the Provisional Government on 24 October.

Source D: From a speech by Trotsky to the Petrograd Soviet, 22 October 1917

The Soviet government will give everything the country has to the poor and to the soldiers at the front ... We will defend the cause of the workers and peasants to the last drop of blood.

Source B: Photograph of Bolsheviks outside the Smolny Institute, Petrograd, October 1917

Source C: From *History of the Russian Revolution*, written by Trotsky in 1932. He was describing his time in the Smolny Institute during October 1917

The Smolny Institute was being transformed into a fortress. In the top floor there were about two dozen machine-guns. All the reports about the movements of troops, the attitude of soldiers and workers, the agitation in the barracks, the happenings in the Winter Palace – all these came to the Smolny.

Tasks

2. *What can you learn from Source B about the Bolsheviks' state of preparation at this time?*

3. *Using the information and sources, explain Trotsky's role in preparing the Bolsheviks in September and October for revolution.*

What were the main events of the Bolshevik Revolution?

Source E: From a letter written by Lenin on the eve of the Bolshevik Revolution. He was urging his colleagues to do what in fact they were doing!

The situation is extremely critical. Delaying the uprising now really means death ... We must at any price, tonight arrest the Ministers and we must disarm the military cadets ... We must not wait! We may lose everything! ... The government is tottering. We must deal it the death blow at any cost.

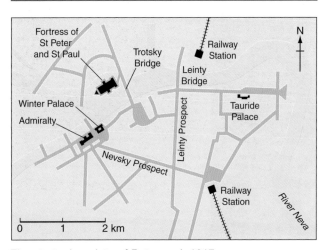

The strategic points of Petrograd, 1917

On the night of 24 October, Trotsky's plans were put into action. Key buildings, such as telegraph offices and railway stations, were captured by the Bolsheviks, and roadblocks were set up on the city's bridges and surrounding the Winter Palace, where the Provisional Government was in session. There was little resistance and the citizens of Petrograd went about their everyday business.

Kerensky escaped from Petrograd on the morning of 25 October and tried to raise troops from the front, while the rest of the government remained in the Winter Palace. He could secure no further help. The troops guarding the Provisional Government – the Women's Battalion (known as the Amazons) and the military cadets – surrendered. When the cruiser *Aurora* sailed up the River Neva and fired its guns, the Provisional Government gave in and was placed under arrest. Some of its members were able to slip away unnoticed. In all, the actions of the day had ended with the death of six soldiers, eighteen arrests and the collapse of the Provisional Government.

A re-enactment of the storming of the Winter Palace in Petrograd, three years to the day after it happened. Do you think this is an accurate representation of what happened, given the events described opposite? If not, why do you think it was re-enacted in this way?

The Bolsheviks take power

Meanwhile, the All-Russian Congress of Soviets was assembling at the Smolny Institute. The Bolsheviks held the most seats – 390 of 650. The SR and Menshevik representatives condemned the Bolshevik takeover, because it was not a Soviet takeover of power. The two sets of representatives left the Congress and the Bolsheviks' position was immediately strengthened because of their huge majority.

The following day, Lenin formed a government called the Council of Peoples' Commissars. This had an all-Bolshevik membership:

- Lenin was the head of the government
- Trotsky was Commissar of Foreign Affairs
- Stalin was Commissar for Nationalities.

Tasks

1. *Study Source E. If Lenin was 'urging his colleagues to do what in fact they were doing!', what can you learn about Lenin at this time?*

2. *Working in groups, can you suggest reasons why there was so little opposition to the Bolshevik takeover in Petrograd in October 1917? Make a list of the reasons – you should see that many of them are also the reasons why there was a Bolshevik Revolution.*

Source F: An artist's interpretation of a poster, dated 5 November 1917, written by Lenin, announcing that the Bolsheviks had removed the Provisional Government

To the Citizens of Russia!

The Provisional Government has been deposed. Power has passed into the hands of the Petrograd Soviet of Workers' and Soldiers' Deputies – the Military Revolutionary Committee, which leads the Petrograd proletariat and the garrison. The causes for which the people have fought – peace, the abolition of land ownership, workers' control over production and the establishment of Soviet power have been secured.

Long live the revolution of the workers, soldiers and peasants!

Why were the Bolsheviks successful?

Source G: From Kerensky's book *The Catastrophe*, written in 1927. Here he is writing about the night of the Bolshevik uprising in October

The hours of the night dragged on painfully. We expected reinforcements from everywhere, but none appeared. There were endless telephone negotiations with the Cossack army regiments … they said they would saddle their horses … meanwhile the hours passed … Not a word from the Cossacks.

Weakness of Provisional Government

The Provisional Government was weak and really only a temporary body. It had not been elected by the people of Russia. Moreover, it had had to share power in Petrograd with the Soviet from the beginning and could not overturn Soviet Order Number One (see page 41).

Kerensky was never able to remove the Bolsheviks completely and during the Kornilov Revolt he had actually armed them. As 1917 unfolded, the Provisional Government was unable to win over the support of ordinary people in Petrograd – the Bolsheviks and other parties were able to publish so much propaganda that when the crisis came in October, Kerensky received little or no help.

Bolshevik control of armed forces

Trotsky claimed that the Bolsheviks were successful because the soldiers of the Petrograd garrison did not side with the Provisional Government. Furthermore, the creation of the Military Revolutionary Committee enabled the Bolsheviks to control some of the armed forces at a critical time.

Lack of alternatives

The many political parties did not offer clear leadership during 1917. They all became discredited because they supported the continuation of the war. This led to discontent within the army and began to make it increasingly unreliable. The elections to the Constituent Assembly were delayed and the peasants' demand for land was not addressed. Consequently, anarchy and the seizing of land in the countryside increased as 1917 wore on, and left-wing agitators infiltrated the army and destroyed the morale of the soldiers.

Role of Lenin

The role of Lenin was crucial. Lenin persuaded the Bolsheviks to oppose the war, unlike the Mensheviks and Socialist Revolutionaries. These two parties were still following Marx's ideas that the workers' revolution was many years away – Lenin had already changed his views in the April Theses (see page 48). He gave the Bolsheviks simple slogans, which were easily understood by the ordinary people:

Lenin had tremendous energy and vitality and his commitment to revolution spurred on the Bolsheviks. His decision to oppose the war was the key reason why Bolshevik support rose throughout 1917. He created the Red Guard and brought German money, which helped to equip them. Lenin persuaded the majority of the Central

Committee to seize power in October. Trotsky organised the takeover, but without Lenin the Bolsheviks would not have even tried to remove the Provisional Government.

Source H: **A cartoon showing Lenin sweeping away his opponents. The caption reads 'Lenin cleans the earth of evil spirits'**

Тов. Ленин ОЧИЩАЕТ
землю от нечисти.

Tasks

1. *After reading this section revisit the balance sheet task you did on page 49. Add to it and then weigh up again whether Lenin's role in the revolution was more important than other factors.*

2. *Working in small groups choose one of the following options and prepare a case for class discussion.*

- *Lenin was the key to Bolshevik success in 1917.*
- *Trotsky was the key to Bolshevik success in 1917.*
- *The mistakes of the Provisional Government were the key to Bolshevik success in 1917.*

Examination practice

How to answer

Make copy of the grid below and complete it to help you plan your answer.

	Agrees with interpretation	Disagrees with interpretation
Source C		
Source D		
Source E		Shows that Lenin was concerned about the military cadets and wanted them disarmed.
Source F		
Source G	Indicates that no forces came to help the Provisional Government.	
Source H		
Own knowledge	Many soldiers were deserting and soldiers in Petrograd were refusing to shoot demonstrators.	The Amazons were thought to be a threat.

1 First of all, study Sources C–H on pages 51–55.
 • Which sources agree with the interpretation? Why? Give a brief explanation in the grid. An example is given above.
 • Which sources disagree with the interpretation? Why? Give a brief explanation in the grid. An example is given above.

2 Now, use your own knowledge of the Bolshevik Revolution.
 To help you, look again at pages 45–55.
 • What knowledge can you use to agree with the interpretation? Summarise this in your grid. An example is given above.
 • What knowledge can you use to disagree with the interpretation? Summarise this in your grid. An example is given above.

Writing your answer

Use the following guidelines.

Introduction

In your introduction explain the two possible sides to the interpretation.

Example

There are various interpretations of the overthrow of the Provisional Government. Some suggest that there was great support from the ordinary people and citizens of Russia. Others indicate that it had more to do with failures of the Provisional Government.

Agree with the interpretation

• First use the sources.

Example

Source G seems to agree with the interpretation because Kerensky infers that he could not rely on parts of the army.

Use your own knowledge here to explain that other parts of the army at the front were deserting.

• Then use your own knowledge to agree with the interpretation.

Example

From my own knowledge (tell the examiner you are using your own knowledge) I agree with the interpretation because the Petrograd garrison was beginning to mutiny and could no longer be relied on.

Disagree with the interpretation

• First use the sources.

Example

In Source E, Lenin seems extremely concerned that there is only a limited time to strike; if he had much support then there was no need to worry.

Can you expand on any facts/dates in the sources to bring in your own knowledge?

• Then use your own knowledge.

Example

From my own knowledge I disagree with the interpretation because the Bolsheviks did not have a huge following in 1917 and Lenin was concerned that they would not win enough seats in the forthcoming elections for the Constituent Assembly.

Conclusion

Your final judgement on the interpretation. Do you mainly agree or disagree? Explain your judgement.

6 Bolshevik rule and its impact, 1918–24

Source A: A Bolshevik poster issued soon after the October 1917 Revolution

Task

What message is Source A trying to get across about the Bolshevik Revolution?

The Bolsheviks had seized power with hardly any bloodshed. The Provisional Government literally melted away and Lenin was left to set up a government. However, the Bolsheviks did not have widespread support across Russia and Lenin was keen to impose his control on the country as soon as was feasible. He faced the same problems as the Provisional Government had and he knew the most pressing issue was Russia's involvement in the war. In attempting to solve his problems, Russia experienced civil war, famine and anarchy in the years to 1921. It was only by 1924, when Lenin dropped some of his Marxist ideas, that Russia returned to some form of stability.

This chapter will answer the following questions:

• How did the Bolsheviks secure control?
• Why was the Constituent Assembly dissolved?
• Why was the Treaty of Brest-Litovsk important?
• Why did a civil war break out in 1918?
• Why did the Bolsheviks win the civil war?
• Why was War Communism important?
• What was the New Economic Policy?

Source skills

The chapter gives you the opportunity to practise the different question types found on Paper 2.

How did the Bolsheviks secure control?

The government that Lenin set up in November 1917 was called *Sovnarkom*, short for Council of Peoples' Commissars. During the weeks after the Bolshevik takeover, soviets throughout Russia joined in the revolution and took over control of most towns and cities. By the end of 1917, nearly all Russia was in soviet hands. This did not mean that Lenin and the Bolsheviks had total control of Russia. Not all the soviets were run by Bolsheviks and, in the countryside, most peasants supported the Socialist Revolutionaries.

Even more awkward from Lenin's point of view, the Provisional Government had arranged for elections to be held in November for a new kind of parliament, called the Constituent Assembly. It seemed that the Socialist Revolutionaries would win more votes than the Bolsheviks. If that happened, the Bolsheviks would have to hand over control of *Sovnarkom* to their rivals.

On top of these problems, Lenin had to keep promises he had openly made in his April Theses (see page 48) – such as giving land to the peasants.

The first decrees of *Sovnarkom*

Sovnarkom, with Lenin as chairman, issued a series of decrees in November and December 1917.

← social

November decrees

DECREE	DESCRIPTION
Decree on land	540 million acres of land taken from the tsar, the nobles, the Church and other landlords. Peasants to set up committees to divide the land fairly
Decree on unemployment insurance	Employment insurance to be introduced for all workers against injury, illness and unemployment
Decree on peace	*Sovnarkom* intended to make peace immediately with Russia's opponents in the war
Decree on work	An eight-hour day and a 40-hour week for all industrial workers to be introduced. There were restrictions on overtime and there was to be holiday entitlement for workers
Decree on titles	All titles and class distinctions were abolished. Women were declared equal to men
Decree on the press	All non-Bolshevik newspapers were banned

December Decrees

DECREE	DESCRIPTION
Decree on workers' control	All factories to be placed under the control of elected committees of workers
Decree to set up the political police	The 'All Russian Extraordinary Commission to fight Counter-Revolution and Espionage' was formed – this became known as the *Cheka*
Decree on political parties	Russia's main liberal party, the Constitutional Democratic Party, was banned
Decree on banking	All banks in Russia came under *Sovnarkom*'s control
Decree on marriage	Couples were permitted to have non-religious weddings and divorce was made easier

Source A: From *The Communist Party of the Soviet Union*, published in 1963. The author, Leonard Schapiro, was describing some of the first actions of the Bolshevik government

Bolshevik practice within a few days of the removal of the Provisional Government was at variance with Lenin's repeated promises. He had said that when they were in power the Bolsheviks would guarantee to each political party which could gather enough supporters the facilities for publishing a newspaper. Some Socialist and Liberal papers, as well as Conservative papers were closed down in the first few days.

Source B: From the Decree on Education, issued by *Sovnarkom* in 1917

Every genuinely democratic power must in the sphere of education, make the removal of illiteracy and ignorance its first aim. It must acquire in the shortest time universal literacy by organising a network of schools and it must introduce universal, compulsory and free tuition for all.

Tasks

1. *What problems did Lenin face when the Bolsheviks first took over in 1917?*

2. *How useful are Sources A and B for a historian in understanding how the Bolsheviks controlled Russia after 1917?*

(Remember how to answer this type of question? For further guidance see pages 37–39.)

3. *Look at the November and December decrees. Copy the table below and fill it in to explain why each section in Russian society would support or oppose the decrees.*

Decree	Worker	Peasant	Middle classes	Nobility

4. *Working in groups, look at the decrees passed by the Bolsheviks in November and December 1917 and discuss the following questions:*

- *Did Lenin follow the April Theses (see page 48)?*
- *In what ways might some people say that Lenin ruled like the tsar?*
- *Was Lenin following the ideas of Marx? (See page 21)*

Why was the Constituent Assembly dissolved?

Elections were held for Russia's new parliament, the Constituent Assembly, in November 1917. They were the first free elections in Russian history.

The Socialist Revolutionaries (SRs) gained more seats in the Assembly than all the other parties put together (see pie chart below).

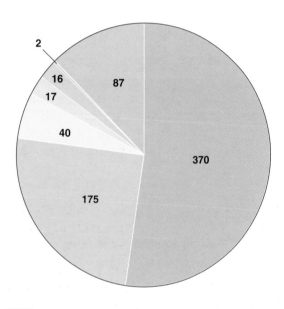

Socialist Revolutionaries

Bolsheviks

Others (representing nationalities)

Left-wing Socialist Revolutionaries

Constitutional Democrats (Cadets)

Mensheviks

Narodniks

Number of seats of different parties in the Constituent Assembly, 1917. Total number of seats was 707.

Lenin was concerned that the Bolsheviks had gained only a quarter of the votes and these were primarily from the working classes of the cities. He was also concerned that some of the nationalities, such as Finns and Estonians, were trying to break away and he wanted to avoid the disintegration of Russia.

Lenin wrote an article for *Pravda*, in which he stated that because there were soviets in Russia, there was no need for the Constituent Assembly.

Nevertheless, the Constituent Assembly met on 18 January 1918. It would have the job of drawing up a new constitution for Russia. The Bolsheviks and the left-wing SRs proposed that the power of the Assembly be limited. When this was defeated, Lenin made his decision to dissolve it.

> **Source A:** From a newspaper article written in 1948 by Victor Chernov, leader of the Socialist Revolutionary Party
>
> *When we, the newly elected members of the Constituent Assembly met on 18 January 1918, we found that the corridors were full of armed guards. Every sentence of my speech was met with outcries, some ironical others accompanied by the waving of guns. Lenin lounged in his chair with the air of a man who was bored to death.*

> **Source B:** From the memoirs of Edgar Sissons written in 1931. Sissons was the US Special Representative in Russia in 1918
>
> *The Constituent Assembly met in a ring of steel. Armed guards were all about us ... a line of guards stood or walked in the connecting corridor, and at every door was a pair of sailors or soldiers. Even the ushers were armed men.*

Photograph of the meeting of the Constituent Assembly in the Tauride Palace, January 1918

Less than twenty-four hours after the assembly had met, Lenin gave the order to dissolve it. Bolshevik Red Guards killed and wounded more than 100 people who demonstrated in support of the Assembly outside the Tauride Palace. Two leaders of the Cadets were killed in a hospital. The Red Guards then prevented the elected Deputies from entering the assembly and closed it down permanently. Lenin had removed a threat to the Bolsheviks and *Sovnarkom* at a stroke.

Source C: From an interview with C. Lindhagen, a Swedish eyewitness at the opening of the Constituent Assembly

In one of the corridors a group of armed soldiers could be glimpsed. I was informed that several of the Deputies (members) as well as the commissars were armed. I asked one of the commissars whether this was true. 'Of course' and he showed me the butt of a revolver in his pocket.

Tasks

1. *Look at the election results in the pie chart on page 60. What can you learn about the political situation in Russia from these results? More information about the different parties can be found on pages 20–21.*

2. *How could Lenin justify dissolving the Constituent Assembly? Write a speech where Lenin explains to the Bolshevik Party why he must dissolve the Constituent Assembly.*

3. *By January 1918, why were some Russians beginning to compare Lenin, unfavourably, with the tsar? Explain your answer carefully.*

4. *Study Sources A, B and C. Does Source C support Sources A and B about the dissolution of the Constituent Assembly?*

(Remember how to answer this type of question? For further guidance see page 23.)

Why was the Treaty of Brest-Litovsk important?

Source A: **German troops with the heaped-up bodies of dead Russian soldiers, early 1918**

Lenin had opposed the war against Germany from the very beginning and much of the support the Bolsheviks had gained came from their opposition to the conflict. He was aware that if the Bolsheviks were to hold on to the power they had won in October 1917, then there would have to be an immediate peace settlement. His greatest concern was that any prolongation of the war would mean that the army would not continue to support him.

Source B: **Decree on Peace, issued by** *Sovnarkom* **in November 1917**

The workers' and peasants' government proposes to all the warring peoples and their governments that they enter immediately into talks for a just peace. This sort of peace would be an immediate one without seizure of foreign territory and without financial penalties.

Peace talks with Germany began on 3 December 1917 and Lenin sent Trotsky (Commissar for Foreign Affairs) as Russia's representative. Talks were held at Brest-Litovsk, near the German border. Trotsky and his negotiating team tried to prolong the talks as long as possible, because they believed that workers in central Europe were on the brink of revolution. When this revolution came, the war would end and then Germany and Russia would make a fair peace.

As the German army advanced into Russia in February 1918, Lenin's hand was forced and he decided to make peace. The terms of the treaty were the harshest possible and Lenin was heavily criticised by many Bolsheviks – for Lenin and Trotsky, Russia's suffering was a small price to pay for the coming **world socialist revolution**.

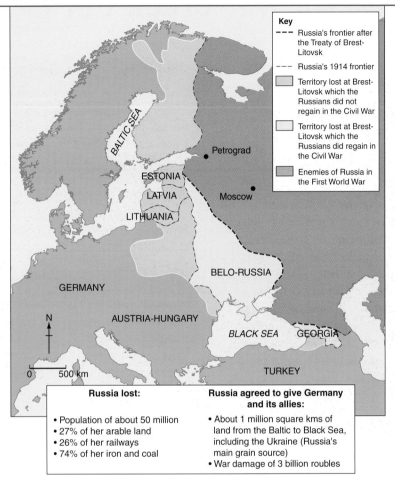

Key

- - - Russia's frontier after the Treaty of Brest-Litovsk
- - Russia's 1914 frontier
▨ Territory lost at Brest-Litovsk which the Russians did not regain in the Civil War
▢ Territory lost at Brest-Litovsk which the Russians did regain in the Civil War
▨ Enemies of Russia in the First World War

Russia lost:	Russia agreed to give Germany and its allies:
• Population of about 50 million • 27% of her arable land • 26% of her railways • 74% of her iron and coal	• About 1 million square kms of land from the Baltic to Black Sea, including the Ukraine (Russia's main grain source) • War damage of 3 billion roubles

Source D: Lenin speaking in March 1918 about the Treaty of Brest-Litovsk

Our impulse tells us to refuse to sign this robber peace ... Russia can offer no physical resistance because she is materially exhausted by three years of war ... The Russian Revolution must sign the peace to obtain a breathing space to recuperate for the struggle.

Lenin won the debate in the Bolshevik Party about the treaty, but only by the narrowest of margins. His gamble paid off, because with the arrival of US troops and the failure of the German **Spring Offensive**, war in Europe was over in the autumn of 1918 and the Treaty of Brest-Litovsk became meaningless. The defeat of Germany now meant that the treaty had no legality.

However, just as the major danger of Germany was removed, Lenin had to face serious internal threats and, by the spring of 1918, Russia was convulsed by **civil war**.

Tasks

1. *Study Sources A and D and the information on pages 62–63. Explain why Lenin was keen to make a peace settlement with Germany.*

2. *Study Sources B and C and use your own knowledge about Russia's involvement in the war to list the reasons why Lenin faced opposition to the signing of the Treaty of Brest-Litovsk.*

Bolshevik rule and its impact, 1918–24

Why did a civil war break out in 1918?

The Russian Civil War lasted for almost three years and involved many groups. Furthermore, it was complicated by the involvement of many foreign countries, all of whom had been Russia's allies in the First World War. The civil war seemed to bring together all the problems of the tsarist years, the First World War and the revolutions of 1917.

The decision to dissolve the Constituent Assembly in 1918 did not win the Bolsheviks any friends. The Social Revolutionaries (SRs) and Cadets accused the Bolsheviks of seizing power by force and demanded the re-calling of the Assembly. They were seeking an opportunity to attack the Bolsheviks. In 1918, open challenges to the Bolsheviks became more common. The SRs tried to seize control of the Moscow Soviet and there were even several assassination attempts on Lenin. Sporadic uprisings across the country encouraged anti-Bolsheviks to come out openly against Lenin's regime.

The desperate economic state of many parts of Russia meant that there was still hunger within the country and this led to growing opposition to the Bolsheviks. The starvation was worsened after the Brest-Litovsk treaty when the Ukraine was lost, as the Ukraine was the main provider of grain for Russia.

The Czech Legion

There is no specific date that marks the start of the civil war but, by May 1918, events escalated when the Czech Legion revolted. Around 50,000 Czechs, who were prisoners of war in Russia, seized control of the Trans-Siberian railway and began to head for Moscow. They attacked the Red Army and were able to drive Bolshevik troops out of Siberia.

The Whites

The collective name for those who opposed the Bolsheviks (the Reds) was the Whites. The Whites had some military support from ex-tsarist officers and were in a position to fight the Bolsheviks – for example, there was General Denikin in the Caucasus, General Yudenich in Estonia and Admiral Kolchak in Siberia. The Czech Legion gave its support to the White generals.

The Greens

The national minorities, for example, the Georgians, saw an opportunity to establish their independence from Russia. If the Bolsheviks were weak and could be attacked on many fronts, then independence was a possibility. Those who fought the Bolsheviks as groups seeking independence from Russia were known as the Greens.

Source A: Map of the Civil War, 1918–21

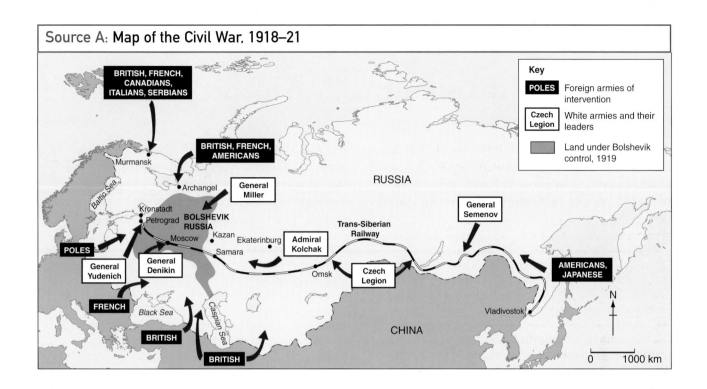

Czech troops on top of an armoured train on the Trans-Siberian railway

Tasks

1. *What can you learn from Source A about the military position of the Bolsheviks in the civil war?*

2. *Draw a concept map to explain and show the links between the causes of the civil war.*

Why did the Bolsheviks win the civil war?

At the start of the war, the Bolshevik (Lenin by this time was using the term Communist) government had to move to Moscow and took desperate protective measures to maintain their power.

From the beginning, the Reds were under pressure. They controlled only a small area of Russia and could see the Whites being supported by foreign powers. But, by early 1919, the tide was turned. The reasons for this are shown below.

Red strengths	White weaknesses
The Reds adopted the policy of War Communism (see pages 68–71), which meant that all necessary resources were poured into the army – even if this meant peasants and workers went hungry	Whites were not united in their approach and operated as separate groups
The Red Army was ably led by Trotsky. Conscription was introduced for men aged 18–40, and Trotsky was given the job of organising the enlarged Red Army. Trotsky's army did not have enough officers and so he cleverly recruited former officers of the tsar's army. There were about 22,000 such officers, who were often blackmailed into fighting for the Bolsheviks. The Red Army eventually had some five million troops	Whites were spread over large areas, whereas the Reds were in a central area with good communications
Peasants would often not support the Whites because they feared that the old tsarist system would be restored – for such people, the Bolsheviks were the lesser of two evils	Morale in the White armies was often low and there were many desertions
The use of the *Cheka* (secret police) terrified ordinary Russians. Those found to have helped the Whites or Greens could expect no mercy. Some estimates put the deaths at the hands of the *Cheka* as high as 50,000 during the civil war. (Estimates for those killed by the Whites are even higher.)	Foreign intervention from Britain, France and the USA was half-hearted and served only to increase support for the Communists

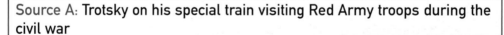
Source A: **Trotsky on his special train visiting Red Army troops during the civil war**

Source B: A selection of Trotsky's orders to the Red Army, 1918

- *Every scoundrel who incites anyone to retreat, to desert, or not fulfil a military order will be shot.*
- *Every soldier of the Red Army who voluntarily deserts his post, will be shot.*
- *Every soldier who throws away his rifle or sells part of his equipment will be shot.*
- *Those guilty of harbouring deserters are liable to be shot.*
- *Houses in which deserters are found are liable to be burned down.*

Source C: A description of the impact of a visit by Trotsky to the front during the civil war. This was written by a member of the Red Army

The town of Gomel was about to fall into the enemy's hands when Trotsky arrived. Then everything changed and the tide began to turn. Trotsky's arrival meant that the city would not be abandoned. He paid a visit to the front lines and made a speech. We were lifted by the energy he carried wherever a critical situation arose. The situation, which was catastrophic twenty-four hours earlier, had improved by his coming – as though by a miracle.

Source D: Bolshevik poster showing the Whites as dogs, on leads held by the **Allied Powers**. The dogs are named Denikin, Kolchak and Yudenich

Tasks

1. *Study Sources A, B and C. Does Source C support the evidence of Sources A and B about the leadership of Trotsky? Explain your answer.*

(Remember how to answer this type of question? For further guidance see page 23.)

2. *Why do you think the Bolsheviks used posters such as that shown in Source D during the civil war?*

3. *How useful is Source D as evidence of the activities of the Whites during the civil war?*

4. *Working in pairs use Sources A, B and C and your own knowledge to list the reasons why the Bolsheviks (Communists) were successful in the civil war.*

Why was War Communism important?

Source A: **A starving peasant family during the famine, 1921**

Task

1. *What can you learn about War Communism from Sources A and B?*

The measures that Lenin and the Communists took to keep the army supplied during the civil war became known as War Communism. Lenin set up the Supreme Council of National Economy (*Vesenkha*) to create a planned economy and a fair society. By the middle of 1918, War Communism meant that the government controlled every aspect of economic life.

The main features of War Communism were:

• Rationing of food in cities was to be strictly applied during food shortages.
• Private trading was banned. Peasants could no longer sell their surplus food for profit but had to give it to the government. Lenin ordered squads into the countryside to seize food if peasants proved unwilling to surrender their produce.
• Factories with more than ten workers were nationalised. This meant that the state now owned the factories. *Vesenkha* decided how much was to be produced in each industry. Workers were under government control and could be told where to work.
• Rapid inflation, which left money valueless. People had to barter, which meant exchanging goods rather than using money.

In theory, Lenin's decision to introduce War Communism was sound, but practically it was flawed. Both workers and peasants objected to it and, as a result, productivity fell (see Source C).

Requisitioning

Source D: From *Memoirs of a Revolutionary* by V. Serge, 1945. Here he is writing about food requisitioning

Groups which were sent into the countryside to obtain grain by requisition might be driven away by the peasants with pitchforks. Savage peasants would slit open a Commissar's belly, pack it with grain, and leave him by the roadside as a lesson to all.

Source E: A White Russian poster of 1919, depicting food requisitioning

Lenin's weaknesses

Source C: Industrial and Agricultural Output, Russia 1913 and 1921

Output in million of tons	1913	1921
Grain	80	37.6
Sugar	1.3	0.05
Coal	29	9
Iron	4.2	0.1
Steel	4.3	0.2
Oil	9.2	3.8
Electricity (in million kWh)	2039	520

Food shortages

War Communism was successful on one level because it supplied the Red Army with food and enabled the victory over the Whites. However, the policy failed to create the **utopian communist state** Lenin hoped for. Peasants did not respond to the idea of giving up produce to the state, and so they grew less and bred fewer animals. The resulting food shortage in 1920 developed into a famine in 1921. It has been estimated that about seven million people died during the famine. There had to be international aid for Russia in the crisis.

A group called Workers' Opposition was formed to press for changes to the policy. One of the group's calls was for 'Soviets without Communists'.

The Kronstadt Rebellion

The greatest challenge for Lenin and Trotsky over War Communism was the Kronstadt Naval Rebellion in 1921. Thousands of sailors protested at events in Russia and objected, like the Workers' Opposition, to the way the Communist Party (the Bolsheviks were now called Communists) was taking power away from the soviets.

Lenin wanted no opposition and decided to stop the protests. Trotsky had to use the Red Army to put down the rebellion and 20,000 men were killed or wounded in the fighting. The surviving rebels were either executed by the *Cheka* or put in a *gulag*. For other opponents, the end of the rebellion meant the end of any hope of removing the Communists.

Lenin realised he had to change the policy – for him, Kronstadt was the 'flash that lit up reality'. In March 1921, Lenin abandoned War Communism and introduced the New Economic Policy in its place.

> ### Tasks
>
> 2. Study Sources A, B and C on pages 68–70. Does the evidence of Source C support Sources B and C about the failures of War Communism?
>
> (Remember how to answer this type of question? For further guidance see page 23.)
>
> 3. How useful are Sources D and E about the effects of food requisitioning during War Communism?
>
> (Remember how to answer this type of question? For further guidance see pages 37–39.)

> **Source F: The political manifesto of the Kronstadt rebels, 1921**
>
> *We joined the Communist Party to work for the good of the people and stand for the help of the workers and peasants. The worker, instead of becoming master of the factory, became a slave ... those who dare to say the truth are imprisoned to suffer the torture cells of the* Cheka *or are shot.*

> ### Tasks
>
> 4. Write an article for Pravda *explaining to the Communist Party why the policy of War Communism failed.*
>
> 5. Why do you think that the Kronstadt Rebellion influenced Lenin to change his economic policy?

What was the New Economic Policy?

Source A: From a speech by Lenin to party members in 1921

We are now retreating, going back as it were, but we are doing this so as to retreat first and then run and leap forward more vigorously. We retreated on this one condition alone when we introduced our New Economic Policy . . . so as to begin a more determined offensive after the retreat.

Task

1. *What can you learn from Source A about Lenin's attitude to the New Economic Policy?*

The New Economic Policy (NEP) was intended by Lenin primarily to meet Russia's urgent need for food. If the peasants could not be forced, then they must be persuaded. He also felt that the new policy would give Russia some breathing space after a period of almost eight years' war. There were some Communists who felt that they were betraying the revolution by reverting back to capitalism.

The NEP said that:

- peasants would still have to give a fixed amount of grain to the government, but they could sell their surplus for profit again
- peasants who increased their food production would pay less tax
- factories with less than 20 workers would be given back to their owners and consumer goods could be produced and sold for profit
- people could use money again and a new rouble was introduced
- key industries, such as coal and steel, still remained under state control.

Trotsky described the New Economic Policy as the 'first sign of the degeneration of Bolshevism'. One rumour had it that the letters NEP stood for 'New Exploitation of the Proletariat'. Those who criticised the NEP said that a new class was created – 'NEPMEN'. This term was applied to those who stood to gain from the capitalism permitted under the new policy: these were the *kulaks*, the retailers and the small manufacturers. It was said that greed and selfishness were returning to Russia. However, there was clearly an economic recovery under the New Economic Policy, as Source B indicates.

Source B: Agricultural and industrial recovery during the New Economic Policy	1921	1922	1923	1924	1925
Agriculture					
Sown area (million hectares)	90.3	77.7	91.7	98.1	104.3
Grain harvest (million tonnes)	37.6	50.3	56.6	51.4	72.5
Industry					
Coal (million tonnes)	8.9	9.5	13.7	16.1	18.1
Steel (thousand tonnes)	183	39	709	1140	2135
Finished cloth (million metres)	105	349	691	963	1688
Value of factory output (million roubles)	2004	2619	4005	4660	7739
Electricity (million Kwhs)	520	775	1146	1562	2925
Rail freight carried (million tonnes)	39.4	39.9	58.0	67.5	83.4
Average monthly wage of urban worker (in roubles)	10.2	12.2	15.9	20.8	25.2

Debate about the NEP continued throughout its existence. However, when Lenin died in 1924, the debate was set to become ever more fierce within the Communist Party.

Source C: Photograph of Nepmen in Smolensk market, 1921

Source D: From the book *From Lenin to Stalin* by Victor Serge, a former Communist. This was written in 1937. Here he was attacking the NEP

In just a few years, the NEP restored to Russia an aspect of prosperity. But to many of us this prosperity was sometimes distasteful . . . we felt ourselves sinking into the mire – paralysed, corrupted . . . There was gambling, drunkenness and all the old filth of former times . . . Classes were re-born under our eyes . . . There was a growing gap between the prosperity of the few and the misery of the many.

Tasks

2. *Study Sources B, C and D. Does Source B support the evidence of Sources C and D about the success of the NEP? Explain your answer.*

(Remember how to answer this type of question? For further guidance see page 23.)

3. *Explain why Trotsky and Serge opposed the New Economic Policy.*

The Rise and Fall of the Communist State: The Soviet Union, 1928–91

A mass grave at Chelyabinsk with the remains of Soviet citizens who died during Stalin's purges of the 1930s. In this outline study you will find out the reasons for this mass grave.

Task

What impression of the Soviet Union do you get from this photograph?

This outline study examines the key developments in the Soviet Union during the years 1928–91. It was a period dominated by four Soviet leaders – Stalin, Khrushchev, Brezhnev and Gorbachev.

Stalin led the Soviet Union from 1928 until his death in 1953. This was a period of great economic change but also of great suffering due to a series of purges and the German invasion of 1941.

In 1956, Stalin's successor, Khrushchev, denounced Stalin's policies and tried unsuccessfully to bring about further economic change.

During Brezhnev's leadership, little was achieved and the Soviet Union did not make progress.

Gorbachev, who became leader in 1985, introduced ambitious reforms in an attempt to solve the problems of the Soviet Union. They had the opposite effect and hastened its break-up.

Each chapter explains a key issue and examines a key line of enquiry as outlined below.

Chapter 7 The nature of Stalin's dictatorship (pages 77–94)
- Who was Stalin?
- Why did Stalin win the leadership contest?
- What was the 'Cult of Stalin'?
- What were the purges?
- What were the effects of the purges?
- Did the position of women change?

Chapter 8 Changes in industry and agriculture under Stalin (pages 95–112)
- Why did Stalin decide to modernise Soviet industry and agriculture?
- What were the Five-Year Plans?
- What results did the Five-Year Plans have?
- Why did Stalin decide on collectivisation?
- What opposition was there to collectivisation?
- What were the effects of collectivisation?
- Were Stalin's economic policies a success?

Chapter 9 The Soviet Union, 1941–53 (pages 113–120)
- Why did the Soviet Union survive the German invasion of 1941?
- What effects did the war have?
- Why did the Cold War begin?
- What were the key features of the period 1945–53?
- What problems did Stalin leave?

Chapter 10 Khrushchev and the Soviet Union (pages 121–132)
- Why did Khrushchev emerge as leader?
- Why was de-Stalinisation introduced?
- What changes were made to industry?
- What changes were made to agriculture?
- Why did Khrushchev fall from power?

Chapter 11 The decline and fall of the communist state (pages 133–149)

- What were the key features of the Brezhnev years?
- Why were there leadership changes between 1982 and 1985?
- Why did the Soviet Union collapse?
- What were Gorbachev's aims and policies?
- Why did Gorbachev's policies fail?
- How did the Communist State collapse?

Outline study questions

There are a number of different types of questions to answer on Paper 1: four in Section (a) and two in Section (b). Below are examples from the June 2005 Paper. Each set of questions is divided into two sections:

Section (a) – short mini essay-type questions (this page)

Section (b) – two essay questions (page 76).

This is a **reason** question. This means you must give one reason and an explanation for it. Another introductory question worth three marks is a **definition** question where you have to explain the meaning of a word or term.

EXAM

PAPER 1   Section (a)

Part (a) of this question is about the Soviet Union in the years 1928 to 1945.

(a)   (i) Give one reason to explain why Stalin introduced the policy of collectivisation.

(3 marks)

(ii) Describe the key features of the policy of collectivisation in the 1930s.

(5 marks)

(iii) Why did Stalin introduce changes to the organisation on industry in the Soviet Union in 1928?

(5 marks)

(iv) In what ways was Stalin successful in his industrial policies in the years to 1941?

(7 marks)

(Total 20 marks)

This is a **key features** question. In this type of question you have to describe the most important events or developments.

This is another **key features** question. In this type of key features question, which asks 'In what ways?', you have to give the key points.

This is a **causation** question. In this type of causation question, which asks 'Why?', you have to give reasons.

PAPER 1

This is known as a **scaffolding** question because the examiner has given you a scaffold (four points) to write about.

Part (b) of this question is about the Soviet Union in the years 1955–1991.

(b) (i) In what ways did Khrushchev try to change Soviet agriculture and industry in the years 1955–64?

You may use the following information to help you with your answer:

De-Stalinisation

Virgin Lands Scheme

Space race

Production of consumer goods.

(15 marks)

(ii) Choose two items from the boxes below and explain why each was important in the decline of the Soviet Union in the years after 1985.

(10 marks)

This is a **ten-mark essay** question. In this type of question you have to make a judgement on the importance of two factors.

Perestroika	1989: collapse of the Berlin Wall	The role of Yeltsin

(Total 25 marks)

Essay writing/planning skills

As you can see, Paper 1 tests not only your knowledge and understanding but your essay-writing skills. Each question is asking you to organise your knowledge to ensure you focus your answer to a particular question. For example, the last question is not asking you to write everything you know about two of these factors. Instead you have to explain the importance of each.

It is therefore important that you get into the habit of:

- planning your answers, especially to the essays in Section (b), before you write
- developing your essay-writing skills.

You will be given advice on all of these questions during the course of Chapters 7–11.

This shows Stalin (middle) next to Yezhov (right)

This shows the same photograph a few years later.

Tasks

Study the two photographs.

1. *What is different about the second picture?*

2. *What do you think might have happened in the meantime? (Answer on page 151.)*

In the 1930s, Stalin established probably the most effective and ruthless dictatorship of the twentieth century. This involved not only a systematic programme of propaganda, culminating in the 'Cult of Stalin', but the removal of any potential threats to his position which, in turn, led to the death of millions of people in the Soviet Union.

This chapter will answer the following questions:

- Who was Stalin?
- Why did Stalin win the leadership contest?
- What was the 'Cult of Stalin'?
- What were the purges?
- What were the effects of the purges?
- Did the position of women change?

Exam skills

In this chapter you will practice the first question in Section (a) of Paper 1. This is a definition or reason question, worth three marks, which can ask you to either:

- explain/define a term
- explain one reason or consequence.

Who was Stalin?

Stalin was born in 1879 in the state of Georgia, the son of a bootmaker. His real name was Joseph Djugashvili. He was from a poor background and had a harsh upbringing. Nevertheless, his mother was determined that he do well and she worked hard to pay for his education. Indeed, he gained a scholarship to a college for training priests in Tiblisi. However, he lost interest in God when he discovered **Marxism** and, in 1899, was expelled from the college.

He greatly admired the writings of Lenin and became a member of the Bolshevik Party (see page 20), taking the name of Stalin, meaning 'Man of Steel'. In the period after 1902, he became an active revolutionary, taking part in over 1000 raids to seize money for the party. He was arrested and exiled to Siberia eight times, escaping on seven occasions.

He was freed from exile in 1917 and returned to Petrograd to become editor of *Pravda*, the Bolshevik newspaper. The evidence suggests he played little role in the **Bolshevik Revolution** of 1917 (see page 49). Nevertheless, he was made **Commissar of Nationalities** in Lenin's government and crushed a rebellion in his own state of Georgia with great brutality. In 1922, he was given what was regarded as the most boring and dull of jobs, General Secretary of the Bolshevik Party, responsible for the day-to-day running of the Party and the appointment and dismissal of key members.

Task

Draw up a brief curriculum vitae for Stalin up to 1922. You could use the headings in the example below, or design your own.

A photograph of Stalin after his arrest in 1902

Curriculum Vitae

Name: Joseph Stalin

Skills

Education

Work experience

Interests

Why did Stalin win the leadership contest?

After Lenin's death in 1924 there was a struggle for power in Russia. There were five possible candidates to succeed Lenin. If you had been able to place a bet on the successful candidate, the odds would have read something like those in the betting shop below. By 1928 Stalin had emerged as leader. Why was the rank outsider successful?

BETTING SHOP

Who will succeed Lenin?

Leon Trotsky

2/1 favourite

He had organised the successful Bolshevik Revolution of 1917 and led the Red Army to victory in the Russian Civil War. He was very intelligent and Lenin's choice as his successor.

Gregory Zinoviev

15/1 outsider

He had helped Lenin to set up the Bolshevik Party in 1903. During Lenin's government he was made the Bolshevik Party boss in Petrograd and was head of the **Comintern**, the organisation through which Soviet Russia tried to bring about Communist revolutions in other countries.

Lev Kamenev

20/1 outsider

Although he angered Lenin by opposing the Bolshevik Revolution of 1917, he was made the leader of the Bolshevik Party in Moscow.

Nikolai Bukharin

25/1 outsider

He was a leading Bolshevik who had opposed the Treaty of Brest-Litovsk by which Russia lost much land to Germany in March 1918. He was a firm supporter of Lenin's **New Economic Policy**.

Joseph Stalin

100/1 rank outsider

He had played little part in the Bolshevik Revolution of 1917. Moreover Lenin, himself, did not want Stalin to succeed him and, in his last testament, tried to warn other leading Bolsheviks about him (see Source A on page 80).

Source A: Lenin's views on Stalin in his testament, 1923

Comrade Stalin, having become Secretary, has unlimited authority concentrated in his hands and I am not sure whether he will be capable of using that authority with sufficient caution. Comrade Trotsky, on the other hand, is perhaps the most capable man in the present Committee. Stalin is too rude and this fault is not acceptable in the office of Secretary. Therefore I propose to comrades that they find a way of removing Stalin from his post.

Source B: A photograph showing Stalin (on the right) as the chief mourner at Lenin's funeral, 1924

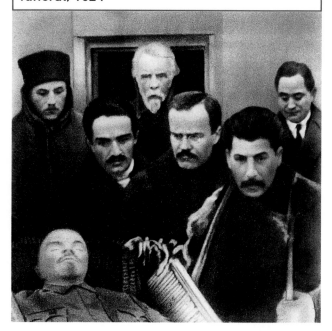

Trotsky's weaknesses

Trotsky was not popular with the *Politburo* and the '**Old Bolsheviks**' because he had not joined the party until 1917, having been a **Menshevik**. Kamenev and Zinoviev disliked Trotsky and disagreed with his political ideas. He also failed to use his popularity in the army to help his cause.

Trotsky believed in permanent or 'world revolution'. He felt that communism would not survive unless the communist revolution spread to other countries. He believed it was the duty of the Soviet Union to help revolutionary groups in other countries. This did not appeal to many Russians, who had experienced four years of war followed by three years of civil war.

Trotsky and the other contenders under-estimated Stalin because he appeared dull and hardworking.

Stalin's strengths

As General Secretary, Stalin held the key post in the Party. He appointed officials who supported him and he removed known supporters of Trotsky in order to build up a strong power base within the Party. He soon commanded the support of most Party officials who owed their position to him.

Stalin successfully presented himself as Lenin's close follower. For example, Stalin appeared as the chief mourner at Lenin's funeral, whilst Trotsky was conspicuous by his absence. Stalin also used propaganda, especially faked photographs, to show how close he was to Lenin and to criticise Trotsky.

Stalin also used clever tactics. He played off one group in the Party against another. At first, in 1925, he worked with Kamenev and Zinoviev against Trotsky and had him expelled from the Party. He then worked with Bukharin against Kamenev and Zinoviev, and had these two expelled. Finally, he turned on Bukharin and had him removed.

Crucially, Stalin's ideas for the future proved more popular with the Party. He promoted 'Socialism in One Country'. He felt that the Soviet Union should concentrate on establishing communism at home, making itself a modern country.

Tasks

1. *Why would the photograph, Source B, help Stalin in his attempts to succeed Lenin?*

2. *Lenin has just died and you are a friend and adviser to Trotsky. Write a letter to Trotsky giving him advice on how he could win the leadership contest.*

Examination practice

Question 1 – reason

Give one reason to explain why Stalin won the leadership contest that followed the death of Lenin.

(3 marks)

This is an example of the introductory question on Paper 1. It is worth three marks.

How to answer
- Focus on the key issue in the question.
- For this question it is *why Stalin won the leadership contest.*
- Begin your answer by giving the reason.

Example
One reason why Stalin won the leadership contest was because of his position as General Secretary of the Communist Party.

- Now give an explanation for this reason. Be as precise as you can in order to achieve the maximum three marks.

Example
Stalin was able to use this position from 1922 to control all major appointments to the Communist Party. He gradually removed known supporters of Trotsky and replaced them with his own supporters, giving himself a strong base of support by 1925.

Question 2 – reason

Now have a go yourself

Give one reason to explain why Trotsky lost the leadership contest that followed the death of Lenin.

(3 marks)

What was the 'Cult of Stalin'?

One of the key features of any **totalitarian state** is to glorify the leader and turn them into an almost god-like being. This 'cult of personality' was developed by Stalin, using the skills of propaganda he had developed as editor of *Pravda*.

How was this achieved?

Stalin's name and picture were everywhere. Streets and cities were named after him and poems and plays were written about him. He created the image of himself as a caring leader whose genius had saved the Soviet Union from its enemies and made it the envy of the world. Huge parades in Red Square in Moscow, films, statues and paintings all showed how fortunate the Soviet people were to have such a great leader.

Artists, writers and film-makers were instructed to produce works in praise of Stalin and his achievements. Ordinary people were told that Stalin was the centre of all that was good and wise. He promised to reward those who were loyal to him with better housing and promotion at work. Party members, such as Audienko in Source B, were forever praising his achievements.

Source A: **Propaganda poster of Stalin from the 1930s**

Source B: **Extract from a speech by A. Audienko, a writer, to the Seventh Congress of Soviets in February, 1935**

Thank you Stalin. Thank you because I am joyful. Thank you because I am well. No matter how I old I become, I shall never forget how we received Stalin two days ago. Centuries will pass, and the generations still to come will regard us as the happiest of mortals, as the most fortunate of men, because we lived in the century of centuries, because we were privileged to see Stalin, our inspired leader.

Tasks

1. *Give one reason to explain why Stalin introduced the 'cult of personality'.*

(This is a reason question. For further guidance see page 81.)

2. *What image does Source A give of Stalin? How does the artist create this image?*

How did Stalin change history?

Stalin had to rewrite history to glorify his own part in the past, especially the Bolshevik Revolution, and remove that of 'enemies' such as Trotsky and other leading Bolsheviks. Photographs, such as the one on page 77, were doctored so that these people disappeared from Soviet history. In this way, images of Bukharin, Zinoviev and Kamenev were eventually removed from photographs.

At the same time, new photographs and histories were created, emphasising Stalin's role, especially his apparent close links with Lenin, who was still treated as a god in Soviet society. Stalin even encouraged the 'Cult of Lenin' but with himself close at hand. Photographs were faked to show Stalin close to Lenin (see Source C).

> **Source C:** A fake photograph. Stalin (right) has been added to this photograph of Lenin, originally taken in 1922

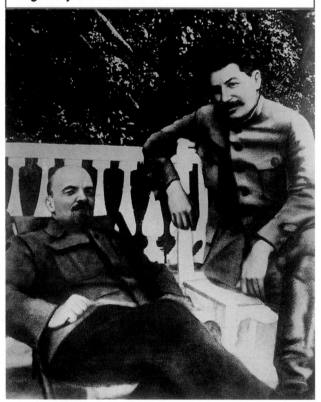

How was culture controlled by Stalin?

Stalin saw writers and artists as dangerous. All their work was carefully censored. It had to be submitted to committees before it was published, as described in Source D.

> **Source D:** From Victor Serge's Memoirs of a Revolutionary, 1945
>
> *Censorship in many forms, mutilated or murdered books. Before sending a manuscript to the publisher, an author would assemble his friends, read his work to them and discuss together whether such-and-such pages would 'pass'. The head of the publishing group would then consult the Gavlit, or Literature Office, which censored manuscripts and proofs.*

This widespread propaganda campaign was directed particularly at children. Children were taught that Stalin was the 'Great Leader'. They learnt Stalin's version of history.

Writers, artists, film-makers and even composers, had to support the government by following the policy of 'Socialist Realism'. This meant that their work had to deal with ordinary working people, show how communism was developing and give simple, clear, optimistic messages.

Tasks

3. *Give one reason to explain why Stalin rewrote history.*

4. *What can you learn from Source D about censorship under Stalin?*

(This is an inference question. For further guidance see page 16.)

5. *You are a Soviet historian asked to rewrite the Bolshevik Revolution of 1917 to greatly enhance the part played by Stalin.*

a. Look at pages 48–53 to see what actually happened.

b. Now rewrite the events of October/November to show that Stalin played a key role. (One possibility could be to substitute Stalin for Trotsky.)

Why were religious groups persecuted?

Religious groups posed a threat to the 'Cult of Stalin' as they owed their allegiance to a different god. Stalin continued the attack on religions after the Bolshevik Revolution:

- Christian leaders were imprisoned and their churches closed down.
- The 'League of the Godless' smashed churches and burned religious pictures.
- Mosques and Muslim schools were closed and pilgrimages to Mecca banned.

Source E: A poster against the Church published in 1932 entitled 'The Kingdom of the Church – A Kingdom in Chains'

What changes were made in education?

This widespread propaganda campaign was directed particularly at children. In 1932, a rigid programme of education was introduced. Discipline was strict and examinations, which had declined since the Bolshevik Revolution, were brought back.

Children were taught that Stalin was the 'Great Leader'. They learnt Stalin's version of history. He even had a new book, *A Short History of the USSR*, written for school students, which gave him a more important role in the revolution. Stalin chose the subjects and information that children should learn. However, he did ensure that by 1939 the majority of Soviet people could read.

Source F: A Russian official describes educational progress in Russia by 1938

During the twenty-one years of the existence of the Soviet Union the aspect of the country has undergone a radical change. A formerly backward and poverty-stricken country has now become an enlightened, cultured and strong socialist power. Half the population are studying in elementary, secondary and higher schools. Illiteracy has now been completely obliterated. In the school year of 1914–15 there were only 155,000 between the ages of eight and eleven years in the schools of Georgia. Now there are 658,000 such school children.

Outside school, Stalin also wanted some control over the young. Children joined political youth groups, which trained them in **socialism** and communism. The youth groups were taught activities such as sports, camping and model-making, and there were different groups for different ages:

- 8–10 year olds joined the Octobrists
- 10–16 year olds joined the Young Pioneers
- 19–23 year olds joined the Komsomol.

Task

6. *What message is the poster, Source E, giving about the Church?*

Source G: The promise made by each member of the Young Pioneers

I, a Young Pioneer of the Soviet Union, in the presence of my comrades, solemnly promise to love my Soviet motherland passionately, and to live, learn and struggle as the great Lenin bade us and the Communist Party teaches us.

Tasks

7. What can you learn from Source F about changes in education under communism?

(This is an inference question. For further guidance see page 16.)

8. Can you trust what this Soviet official has written in Source F? Explain your answer.

9. Why do you think Young Pioneers would have to make this promise?

What was the new constitution of 1936?

In 1936, Stalin introduced a new constitution. This was to convince Soviet citizens and the outside world that the USSR was a 'free' society. In fact, it confirmed Stalin's dictatorship. The USSR now consisted of eleven republics. The Congress of the Soviets of the USSR became the **Supreme Soviet** or parliament of the USSR, with two chambers (sections) instead of one. Elections were to be held by secret ballot.

The Communist Party kept its close control of both the central government and the government of each republic. Stalin held the posts of General Secretary of the Party, Chairman of the *Politburo* and Prime Minister.

Examination practice

Question 1 – definition
What was meant by the 'Cult of Stalin'?

(3 marks)

This is an example of the other type of introductory question on Paper 1 in which you are asked to explain the meaning of a term. It is worth three marks.

How to answer
• Give a precise definition of the term

Example
The 'Cult of Stalin' was Stalin's method of making the people of the Soviet Union believe he was a god-like figure.

• Explain the term by putting it in the context of the time.

Example
Stalin was determined to ensure the support of the Soviet people and used his huge propaganda machine to create this cult through huge parades in Red Square, films, statues and paintings – all of which showed how fortunate they were to have a leader like Stalin.

Question 2 – definition
Now have a go yourself
What was meant by 'Socialist Realism'?

(3 marks)

What were the purges?

In the 1930s, Stalin embarked on a series of **purges,** which lead to the death and imprisonment of millions of Soviet people. No one was immune.

Stalin purged anyone who held up, criticised or opposed his plans for **collectivisation** and **industrialisation** (see page 96). Most of the accused were deported or imprisoned. Some were shot. The first victims were managers and workers accused of wrecking the first **Five-Year Plan,** *kulaks* accused of opposition to collectivisation and ordinary party members accused of incorrect attitudes.

1928
55 engineers from Shakhty mines in Donbas were put on trial accused of sabotage, with five shot and 49 imprisoned.

1932
Ryutin, a senior member of the Communist Party, criticised Stalin's economic policies. A furious Stalin had Ryutin and his supporters arrested and put on trial. Ryutin was expelled from the Party and sent into exile.

1934
Following the murder of Kirov (see page 89), thousands of Communist Party members were arrested, 40,000 in Leningrad alone.

1935
Senior Communists were arrested: 1108 out of 1966 delegates to the 17th Congress; 98 out of 139 members of the Central Committee. Party branches were told to root out anyone who had supported Trotsky. Thousands were denounced and expelled.

1936
The 'show trials' of the 'old Bolsheviks' (see page 91). Zinoviev, Kamenev and other Left Opposition leaders were arrested and confessed to plotting after **NKVD** (secret police) torture and brainwashing.

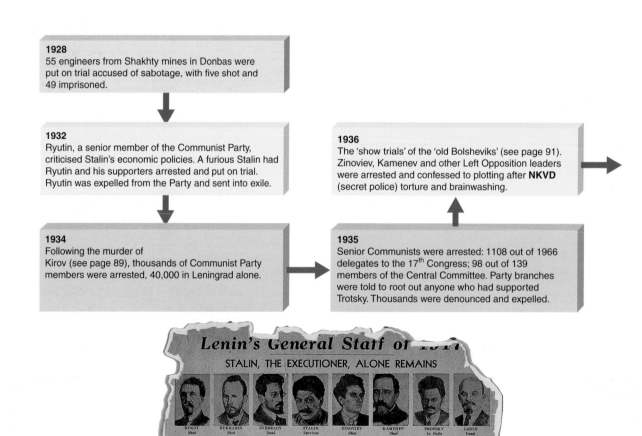

A photograph of 1936 from an American newspaper showing the leading Bolsheviks purged by Stalin

Popular stories/jokes used during the purges

Question: Why do the secret police always travel in threes?
Answer: One can read, one can write and the third is there to keep an eye on the two intellectuals.

A flock of sheep was stopped by frontier guards at the border with Finland.
'Why do you want to leave Russia?' the guards asked.
'It's the NKVD,' replied the terrified sheep. 'Beria (Chief of Police) has ordered them to arrest elephants.'
'But you're not elephants!' the guards exclaimed.
'Yes,' said the sheep, 'but try telling that to the NKVD.'

A man, sitting in his flat, heard a loud knock at the door.
'Who is it?' he asked anxiously.
'It is the Angel of Death.'
'Phew!' the man exclaimed. 'For a moment I thought it was the secret police!'

1937
Stalin was determined to remove any possible opposition in the Red Army and ensure total obedience. The Commander-in-Chief, Marshall Tukhachevsky, and seven other generals were arrested and shot. Tukhachevsky had had serious disagreements with Stalin during the Russian Civil War of 1918–21. In addition, the commanders of the armed forces could be powerful enough to overthrow Stalin. By 1941, almost 90 per cent of all Soviet generals had been purged.

1938
By this year, almost every party and state leader in every one of the Soviet republics had been purged. Stalin called a halt to the purges, which were getting out of hand. He blamed the secret police, which itself was purged to remove all knowledge of what happened. This purge included Yezhov (see page 90).

1940
Trotsky was murdered by one of Stalin's agents in Mexico in 1940.

Source A: A French cartoon of the late 1930s, which shows Stalin controlling the purges

Tasks

1. *Give one reason to explain why Stalin purged the army.*

(Remember how to answer this type of question? For further guidance see page 81.)

2. *Look at the key feature on jokes made during the purges. Can you make up your own joke? (One possibility is a 'knock, knock' type joke.)*

3. *Study Source A.*
a. *What message is the cartoonist trying to get across?*
b. *How does the cartoonist achieve this?*

4. *How useful is Source A as evidence of Stalin's purges?*

(This is a utility question. For further guidance see pages 37–39.)

Why did Stalin introduce the purges?

There was not one reason why Stalin introduced the purges. Indeed, a number of theories and explanations have been given.

1. Threats to his position

Stalin was concerned that his enemies were plotting to overthrow him. His real motive may have been to destroy any men who might form an alternative government – especially the 'Old Bolsheviks'.

> **Source B: Bukharin speaking in 1936**
>
> *Stalin is convinced that he is greater than everyone else. If someone speaks better than he does, that man is for it. Stalin will not let him live, because that man is a constant reminder that he, Stalin, is not the first and best. He is not a man but a devil.*

3. Links with economic policies

One theory argues that it was the only way Stalin could get mass forced labour for his industrial projects. The purges were also a convenient way of excusing setbacks. For example, failures to achieve targets under the Five-Year Plans (see page 98) could be blamed on sabotage rather than faults in the Plan.

Stalin was convinced that he was the only person who could transform the Soviet Union into a modern, industrialised country and that it had to be done quickly. He was convinced that Hitler would attack the USSR and that it would lose the war if it could not produce enough armaments. Any person who tried to stop him accomplishing this great task was, in Stalin's eyes, a traitor.

Reasons for the purges

2. Stalin not totally responsible

Others believe that once the purges started they had a snowball effect and were difficult to stop. Stalin may have started them but lost control at local level where they were often used by unscrupulous people to get rid of rivals or those in a coveted superior position.

4. Persecution complex

Some writers, including a British writer C. P. Snow, believe Stalin was suffering from a persecution complex – that he feared everyone was plotting against him. The murder of Kirov is an example of this.

A newspaper front page of 1940 showing Trotsky after the assassination

The murder of Kirov

Stalin decided that his popular *Politburo* colleague, Kirov, was a possible rival. Kirov, a leading communist, spoke at the Seventeenth Party Congress in 1934. He criticised Stalin's policy on industrialisation and insisted that it should be slowed down. Kirov's speech was warmly applauded and there was even talk of him replacing Stalin as leader.

He was murdered, probably on Stalin's orders. Stalin claimed the murder was part of a plot against him and the Party. The secret police arrested thousands of Kirov's supporters.

Kirov speaking at the Seventeenth Party Congress, 1934

Source C: Vladimir Alliluyev, Stalin's nephew, wrote in 1990 *Stalin, a Time for Judgement*, and insisted his uncle was not involved with the murder

Stalin had nothing to do with that murder. My mother was with him when they phoned and informed him that Kirov had been murdered. And my mother said to me, neither before nor after it had she ever seen Stalin in the state he was in after receiving that phone call. And Stalin knew full well that the murder would be linked with his name.

Source D: Olga Shatunovskaya, who was a member of the commission that inquired into Kirov's death, thought differently

The secret police latched on to the idea that Stalin was dissatisfied after he wrote them a letter saying:

'I am ready for anything now. I hate Kirov.'

And they organised the murder. Of course when Stalin found out that some senior Party members had asked Kirov to become leader, he decided to remove him.

Tasks

5. Give one reason to explain why Stalin carried out the purges.

(Remember how to answer this type of question? For further guidance see page 81.)

6. Does Source D support the evidence of Source C about who was responsible for the murder of Kirov? Explain your answer.

(This is a cross-referencing question. For further guidance see page 23.)

7. Organise the explanations for the purges under the following categories. Do some fall under more than one category? Why might this be the case.

Economic	Political	Psychological

a. Rank order the reasons given for the purges, starting with the most convincing and finishing with the least convincing.

b. Explain your reasons for the first and last in your rank order.

The instruments of the purges

The purges were implemented by the secret police and many of those purged ended up in labour camps known as *gulags*.

The secret police

Lenin set up his own secret police known as the *Cheka*, which was renamed the **OGPU** in 1922. In 1934, its name was changed again to the **NKVD**.

Stalin expanded the secret police and gave it greatly increased powers with the 'decree against terrorist acts', issued after Kirov's murder. This meant they could arrest people without charge or trial and execute them on the spot.

The secret police were sent out at night and were nicknamed the 'black ravens', because they drove round in black cars. They liked to call in the early hours of the morning.

They were assisted by an army of informers. Even children were encouraged to inform on their parents, neighbours and school friends. Informing on others was a way of showing your loyalty, of settling old scores and of getting someone else's more senior job or position.

The NKVD was used by Stalin to hunt down and destroy his opponents and terrorise ordinary people into obedience. People found guilty of opposition or disobedience were sentenced to death, exile or hard labour. The most notorious head of the secret police was Yezhov who, himself, was purged in 1938.

The labour camps

Victims of the purges were sent to the *gulags*, which were set up in Siberia and the Arctic north. They were run by the secret police. Millions of people were imprisoned and forced to do hard manual work on construction and mining projects. About thirteen million died from cold, hunger and ill-treatment. Living conditions were appalling and food supplies totally inadequate. In 1928, there were around 30,000 prisoners in the labour camps. By 1938, it was around seven million.

Source E: From the *Gulag Archipelago* written in 1973 by Alexander Solzhenitsyn. He served time in a labour camp for eight years in the 1940s

In 1938 Ivanor Razannik found 140 prisoners in a cell intended for 25 – with toilets so overburdened that prisoners were taken to the toilet only once a day, sometimes at night. He calculated that for weeks at a time there were three persons per square yard of floor space. In this 'kennel' there was neither ventilation nor a window and the prisoners' body heat and breathing raised the temperature to 40 degrees centigrade. Their naked bodies were pressed against one another and they got eczema from one another's sweat. They sat like that for weeks . . . and were given neither fresh air nor water – except for gruel and tea in the morning.

Gulag prisoners working on the Belomar Canal in 1931. They were expected to do the basic labouring jobs.

Tasks

8. What was meant by the 'gulags'?

(Remember how to answer this type of question? For further guidance see page 85.)

9. Solzhenitsyn was writing about the gulags in a novel. Is Source E still useful as evidence of life in the gulags even though it is fiction? Explain your answer.

What were the 'show trials'?

Source F: A cartoon of the mid-1930s from an American newspaper showing leading Bolsheviks at the 'show trials'

The 'show trials' began in 1936. In that year, Stalin began purging the Communist Party of anyone who might oppose him, especially 'Old Bolsheviks', such as Kamenev and Zinoviev. Along with fourteen others, they were accused of organising the murder of Kirov and plotting to assassinate Stalin.

The accused were put on trial in full view of the world. They were forced to confess to a whole range of amazing crimes, including a plot to murder Lenin. The confessions were important because they showed that Stalin was right to purge the Communist Party. Trotsky, who was now in exile, was accused of being the leader of the plot.

Why did they confess to such crimes?

Such confessions did not help the accused, as they were executed after the trials. They confessed for a number of reasons. First, because they were physically and psychologically tortured by the secret police (see Source H). Second, because their families were threatened with imprisonment or death.

Source G: From Fitzroy MacLean, a British diplomat who observed the show trials

The prisoners were charged with every possible crime including high treason, murder, spying and all sorts of sabotage. They were accused of plotting to wreck industry and agriculture, to assassinate Stalin and break up the Soviet Union. Some were accused of betraying the Soviet cause even before the Bolshevik Revolution of 1917. One after another, using the same words, they admitted their guilt. And yet what they said seemed to bear no relation to reality.

Source H: From Evgenia Ginsburg, who was tortured and wrote an account in *Into the Whirlwind* in 1968

They started to work on me again. I was put on the 'conveyor belt'. The interrogators worked in shifts. I didn't. Seven days without sleep or food. Relaxed and fresh, they passed before me as a dream. The object of the 'conveyor' is to wear out the nerves, weaken the body, break resistance, and force the prisoner to sign whatever is required. Others confessed for the sake of their families and some, most especially Bukharin, confessed as a last service to the Communist Party.

Tasks

10. *What point is the cartoonist trying to get across in Source F?*

11. *How does the cartoonist achieve this?*

12. *What was meant by the 'show trials'?*

(Remember how to answer this type of question? For further guidance see page 85.)

13. *Imagine you are a British witness to one of these trials. Write out a text for a friend describing what you have seen. You have a maximum of 160 letters.*

What were the effects of the purges?

The purges did ensure total control under Stalin, with the removal of any potential rivals to his leadership. However, they had a devastating effect on the Soviet Union.

The human cost was enormous. It is impossible to know how many were killed or imprisoned. However, in 1988 the **KGB** – the name for the secret police at that time – allowed some NKVD files to be examined. This revealed the following figures for 1937–38:

FATE	NUMBER OF PEOPLE
Executed	1 million
Died in labour camps	2 million
In prison, late 1938	1 million
In labour camps, late 1938	8 million

Source A: A photograph of a mass grave at Cheliabinsk in the Urals taken in 1938

The USSR was seriously weakened with the loss of its senior officers in the army and navy. This almost led to defeat in 1941 when Hitler's armies invaded.

The purges undermined much of Stalin's earlier work of building up industry (see page 98). Able scientists, administrators and engineers were arrested, executed or imprisoned, which affected the quality of what was being produced.

Every part of Russia was affected. No village, no home, not even Stalin's own family could escape. His cousins and in-laws were victims of **the Terror**. Anyone could receive a knock on the door in the middle of the night and be dragged away by the secret police.

No one felt secure. Some people took advantage to denounce neighbours or workmates and get their jobs. All trust disappeared. Eventually, the secret police had files on half the urban population in the Soviet Union.

Many were unfairly expelled from the Communist Party. This often had cruel consequences. Without the party card it was impossible to get a job. This punished the whole family. When both parents of one 13-year-old girl were arrested she was forced to live on the streets. In order to survive she had to tell the Young Pioneers (see page 84) that her parents were spies and deserved to be shot.

Source B: Osip Mandelstam, a poet who was arrested in 1934, on the effects of the purges

Everybody seemed intent on his daily round and went smilingly about the business of carrying out his instructions. It was essential to smile – if you didn't it meant you were afraid or discontented. This nobody could afford to admit – if you were afraid, you must have a bad conscience. Everyone had to strut around wearing a cheerful expression as though to say:

'What's going on is no concern of mine. I have important work to do and I'm terribly busy. I am trying to do my best for the State, so do not get in my way'.

The subject nationalities

Stalin was from Georgia, an area that had long wanted self-government and even independence. Unlike Lenin, however, Stalin had no sympathy with these national groups. In the 1930s, a policy of '**Russification**' attempted to impose Russian culture on the USSR. Russian became compulsory in schools and key jobs went to Russians. Army recruits were sent away from their homelands and forced to mix with other ethnic groups. Many who opposed this were purged.

Tasks

1. *Study Source A. Why do you think that the bodies were buried in mass graves?*

2. *What can you learn from Source B about the effects of the purges on everyday life?*

(This in an inference question. For further guidance see page 16.)

3. *What message is the cartoonist trying to get across in Source C?*

4. *Using a concept map show the effects of the purges. You may wish to use the following categories – military, political, economic, social and psychological.*

- *Using a different colour, show on your concept map any links between the effects.*

- *Explain at least one of your links.*

An example of how you could start your concept map is given below.

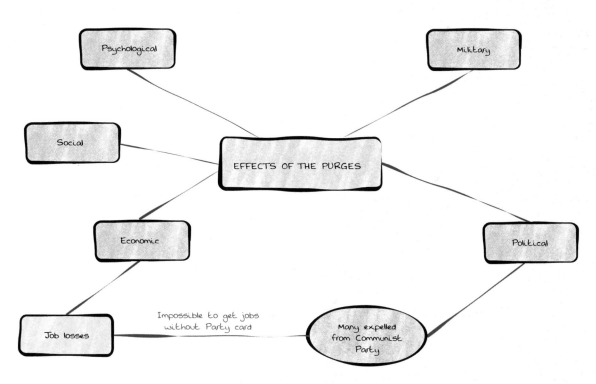

The nature of Stalin's dictatorship

Did the position of women change?

Traditionally in Russia, and certainly before the Bolshevik Revolution of 1917, women were seen as second-class citizens with few rights. There were some changes under Lenin, with marriage and divorce made easy. Both parties simply had to agree and fill in a register. Abortion was made freely available on demand. There was greater equality for women in the workplace.

Family life

However, by the mid-1930s, the family was back in favour and divorce and abortion were less popular. The high divorce rate of the 1920s and early 1930s had created a great number of broken homes and homeless children who lived on the streets begging and robbing. Through propaganda, such as articles in Source A, the state tried to encourage families to stay together – for example, by:

- paying child allowances for married couples
- making divorce much harder
- restricting abortion.

> **Source A: An extract from an article in _Pravda_ in 1936**
>
> _When we talk of strengthening the Soviet family we mean to fight against wrong attitudes towards marriage, women and children. 'Free love' and a disorderly sex life have nothing in common with Socialist principles or the normal behaviour of a Soviet citizen. The outstanding citizens of our country, the best of Soviet youth, are almost always devoted to their families._

Employment

Women continued to make progress in the area of employment. They were encouraged to work in almost all areas. Some women took on jobs like engineering, which had once been done only by men. However, life remained hard for most Soviet women. They were expected to work full time, as well as bring up a family. Help was provided by state nurseries and crèches.

Source B: Government poster of the 1930s

The slogan reads 'The wide development of a network of crèches, kindergartens, canteens and laundries will ensure the participation of women in Socialist reconstruction'

Political position

Politically, women still remained second-class citizens. Less than 20 per cent of the Communist Party was made up of women. Very few women rose to high positions in the Party or government.

Tasks

1. _Give one reason to explain why the position of women changed under Stalin._

(Remember how to answer this type of question? For further guidance see page 81.)

2. _Study Source B. What message is the government trying to get across in this poster?_

3. _Draw a table like the one below and complete it using the information on women._

Progress	Lack of progress

4. _Overall, do you think women made progress under Stalin? Explain your answer._

Changes in industry and agriculture under Stalin

Task

What can you learn from Source A about Stalin's aims for industrialisation?

Stalin was determined to modernise the Soviet economy. He introduced a series of Five-Year Plans that transformed industry and a policy of collectivisation, which brought major changes to agriculture. He sought to develop his own policy of 'socialism in one country', which he felt would benefit the USSR more than Trotsky's policy of world revolution which seemed to offer only continued war and instability.

In this chapter you will be looking at Stalin's attempts to modernise the economy of the Soviet Union through examining the following questions:

- Why did Stalin decide to modernise Soviet industry and agriculture?
- What were the Five-Year Plans?
- What results did the Five-Year Plans have?
- Why did Stalin decide on collectivisation?
- What opposition was there to collectivisation?
- What were the effects of collectivisation?
- Were Stalin's economic policies a success?

Source A: Propaganda painting entitled 'Higher and higher' produced in 1934. Stalin used the phrase 'there is no fortress that we Bolsheviks cannot storm'

Exam skills

This chapter gives guidance on answering the key features style of question on Paper 1. The amount of marks available for this question can be five, seven or ten. It also gives guidance in answering the seven-mark causation question in Section (a) of Paper 1. There are some 'Why . . .?' questions, as well as the descriptive type – 'In what ways . . .?'

Why did Stalin decide to modernise Soviet industry and agriculture?

Source A: From a speech by Stalin in February 1931. He was talking about the backwardness of the Soviet Union

We must create in our country an industry which would be capable of re-equipping and organising the whole of our industry but also our transport and agriculture. The history of Russia shows that because of her backwardness she was constantly defeated. Those that fall behind get beaten. No, we refuse to be beaten. We are 50 and 100 years behind the advanced countries. We must make good this distance in ten years. Either we do it, or we shall be crushed.

Task

1. *What can you learn from Source A about Stalin's aims for the Soviet Union?*

Stalin wanted to transform the USSR from a backward agricultural country to a modern industrial one. His rationale was based on a combination of economic and political factors that were linked by a fear of foreign invasion. Furthermore, he believed that if the Soviet Union was to compete with the industrialised nations of the world, then the only way to do this was by state intervention. He was also aware that any intervention by the state in agriculture and industry would lead to greater control over the people of the Soviet Union.

A set of targets was drawn up in 1928 for each Soviet industry and they had to be met within five years (hence the term Five-Year Plan). Stalin made it clear that workers would have to accept personal sacrifices in the pursuit of these targets. He also put forward reasons why modernisation had to take place.

Fear of invasion

The help given by Britain, France and the USA to the Whites during the civil war of 1918–21 (see pages 64–71) seemed to confirm Stalin's fears of an attack from the West. Industrialisation was essential if the Soviet Union was to ensure victory in any future war. It would enable him to build up and control the armed forces. There were several war scares in the USSR in the late 1920s and there was a growing feeling of **diplomatic isolation** among many leading politicians. Industrialisation would strengthen the country and hopefully deter any would-be opponent.

Disappointing output

Economically, despite the advances made by the New Economic Policy (see pages 72–73), Soviet industrial production remained disappointing. In the 1920s, Soviet production of coal and steel was behind that of France. Central direction and control would enable the government to direct the economy and ensure a rapid expansion in heavy industry in order to outstrip the developed nations.

Communist principles

Stalin also had political reasons. By creating and sharing wealth among the Soviet people he hoped to create a strong state based on communist principles, where the state controlled economic activity. Industrialisation would guarantee the survival of the communist revolution by creating many more members of the proletariat, the backbone of the revolution. It would replace the hated Nepmen – private owners and traders created by the New Economic Policy.

Leadership

Furthermore, industrialisation would consolidate Stalin's position as leader and give him total control of Russian industry. The **right-wing** members of the Communist Party's *Politburo*, Bukharin, Tomsky and Rykov, were in favour of keeping the New Economic Policy. The launching of the Five-Year Plans would enable Stalin to discredit and remove these leading figures and, by 1929, he felt more secure in his position as leader of the Party.

Tasks

2. *You have been given several reasons for Stalin's policy of industrialisation. Draw a concept map showing these motives and try to make links between some of the reasons. An example has been given opposite.*

3. *Which one of the motives behind industrialisation do you think is the most important? Explain your answer.*

4. *Study Source A on page 96 and B on this page. Why do you think Stalin had to rely on propaganda to promote the Five-Year Plans?*

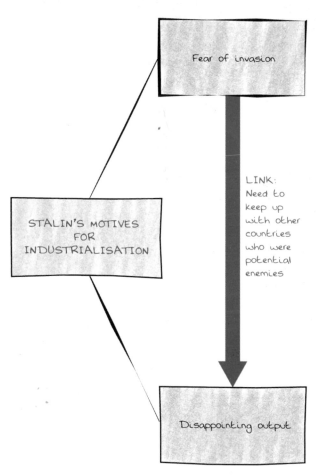

Fear of invasion

STALIN'S MOTIVES FOR INDUSTRIALISATION

LINK: Need to keep up with other countries who were potential enemies

Disappointing output

Changes in industry and agriculture under Stalin

What were the Five-Year Plans?

Source A: **Photograph of the first tractor produced at the Stalingrad Tractor Works in 1930. Tractors would contribute to agricultural improvements. Stalin needed foreign currency from the sale of agricultural produce**

The First Five-Year Plan, 1928–32

In 1928, the NEP was abandoned and the first Five-Year Plan was launched. Industrialisation was to be directed by *Gosplan* (the State Planning Authority), which set targets for certain key industries and ensured that these industries were given priority in the allocation of manpower and raw materials.

The targets that were set were often very unrealistic and Stalin's response to those who said that the pace of industrialisation was too fast was ' …those who lag behind are beaten'.

The first Five-Year Plan (1928–32) concentrated on heavy industry, such as coal, steel and iron. The 'new' industries, such as electricity, motor vehicles, chemicals and rubber, were also targeted but consumer industries, such as textiles and household goods, were neglected.

Key Term

Gosplan

The State Planning Authority. An organisation that was run by the Communist Party. It was given the task of planning the industrialisation of the USSR under the Five-Year Plans. *Gosplan* set targets for industries and allocated resources.

Stalin was encouraged by the apparent success of the plan and he revised targets twice – the table in Source B shows the original and revised targets alongside the actual figures.

Thousands of Soviet citizens, especially young people, went willingly to work in the new towns and factories, because they genuinely believed that they were creating a new society.

Source B: **Table showing industrial output during the first Five-Year Plan**

Production (in million tonnes)	1927-28 Original targets	1932-33 'optimal' (highest expected)	1932 revised targets	1932 actual output
Coal	35.0	75.0	95–105	64.0
Oil	11.7	21.7	40–55	21.4
Iron Ore	6.7	20.2	24–32	12.1
Pig Iron	3.2	10.0	15–16	6.2

Task

1. *What can you learn from Source B about industrial production in the first Five-Year Plan?*

(This is an inference question. For further guidance see page 16.)

Second Five-Year Plan, 1933–37

The Second Five-Year Plan, did, at first, set targets for the increased production of consumer goods. Some of the mistakes of the first plan, such as setting too high targets, were avoided. As fears of invasion from the West increased, especially from Nazi Germany, heavy industry again became the priority. During the second plan, the production of armaments trebled.

Living standards did not increase and strikes were not permitted.

The Third Five-Year Plan, 1938–41

This was launched in 1938, but was abandoned when Germany invaded the Soviet Union in June 1941. It concentrated on the production of household goods and luxuries, such as bicycles and radios.

The following figures are drawn from the work of the economic historian, E. Zaleki, whose findings are based on careful analysis of Soviet and Western sources. They give an overview of industrial production during the Five-Year Plans.

Source C: Table showing industrial output during the Five-Year Plans

Production (in million tonnes)	1927	1930	1932	1935	1937	1940
Coal	35	60	64	100	128	150
Steel	3	5	6	13	18	18
Oil	12	17	21	24	26	26
Electricity	18	22	20	45	80	90

Examination practice

In the examination you will be asked to answer a question, which says

'Describe the key features of . . .'

For this type of question, you need to have some knowledge of the subject and you must explain and develop your answer carefully.

For example, consider the following question.

Question 1 – key features

Describe the key features of the Five-Year Plans.
(7 marks)

How to answer

Plan your answer by listing the relevant points you need to cover. The main question word is 'describe' and in this question the topic is the Five-Year Plans.

Therefore, write about:

- industrialisation
- *Gosplan* and targets
- the focus of each plan.

There are only three points but you need to write about each one. You may wish to start by using the words of the question:

'The key feature of the Five-Year Plans was a focus on industry which meant . . .'

Task

2. Write a newspaper article about the Five-Year Plans, with the headline 'Stalin introduces revolutionary plans to modernise the Soviet Union'.

What results did the Five-Year Plans have?

Advances in industry

Although the plans' targets were not all met, all Soviet industries made remarkable advances and, by 1940, the USSR was the world's second largest industrial power behind the USA. The second Five-Year Plan made greater use of technical expertise, with spectacular growth in the coal and chemical industries. However, oil production, remained disappointing.

In the workplace, employees were urged to work harder through encouragement and the example of people such as the miner Alexei Stakhanov (see photo below). Other workers were encouraged to follow Stakhanov's example and they formed '**shock brigades**' in attempts to copy their worker hero. The **Stakhanovites**, as they were known, were rewarded with medals (the Order of Lenin or Hero of the Soviet Union), new houses, free holidays and other benefits. However, the campaign was quietly dropped in the late 1930s after a number of Stakhanovites were beaten up and killed by their fellow workers.

Stakhanovites

Alexei Stakhanov explaining his working methods to fellow miners. Alexei Stakhanov became a hero of the Soviet Union when, on the night of 30–31 August 1935, it was claimed that he shifted 102 tonnes of coal, which was almost fifteen times the normal amount for a single shift. It was, however, a set-up. He had two helpers who removed the coal while he worked at the coalface with his pick.

Tasks

1. *Why do you think Stalin considered the Stakhanovites to be so important?*

2. *What can you learn from Sources A and B about the construction of new towns in the Soviet Union during the 1930s?*

(This is an inference question. For further guidance see page 16.)

3. *In what ways had the Five-Year Plans changed Soviet industry by 1941?*

(Remember how to answer this type of question? For further guidance see page 105.)

4. *What was meant by the term Stakhanovite movement?*

(Remember how to answer this type of question? For further guidance see page 85.)

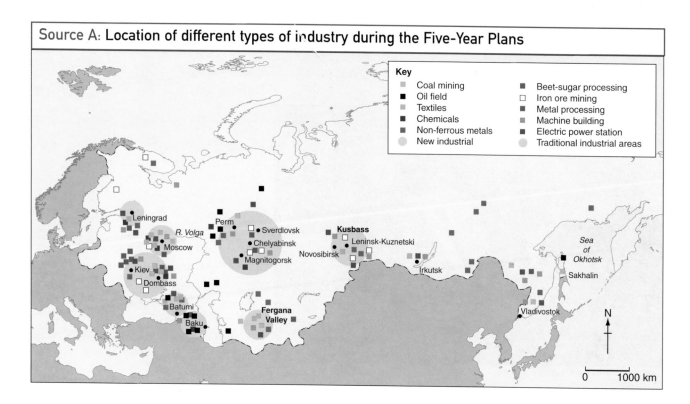

Source A: Location of different types of industry during the Five-Year Plans

Key

- Coal mining
- Oil field
- Textiles
- Chemicals
- Non-ferrous metals
- New industrial
- Beet-sugar processing
- Iron ore mining
- Metal processing
- Machine building
- Electric power station
- Traditional industrial areas

Changes in location and organisation of industry

As can be seen from Source A, much industry was located in the remoter areas of the USSR, east of the Ural Mountains, where industry would be safe against attack from the West. Huge towns and industrial centres were built from scratch deep inside the USSR. For example, Magnitogorsk concentrated on iron and steel. Little had existed there before the Five-Year Plan and workers were either encouraged to move to the site or forced to. In the space of three years, 1929–32, Magnitogorsk grew from 25 to 250,000 people.

In the years 1929–39, the population of the USSR's cities rose by 29 million. Vast construction projects were undertaken, such as the Dnieper Dam hydroelectric power station, the Belomor Canal, the Moscow underground and the Moscow-Volga canal.

Source B: Komsomol volunteers at a construction site at the new city of Komsomolsk, Siberia in the 1930s

МЫ ИДЕМ В ЗАБОЙ!

Changes in industry and agriculture under Stalin

A skilled workforce

Source C: **Soviet girls and women learning to read in a state-run literacy class in the 1930s**

In 1929, Soviet workers lacked many of the skills needed to carry out industrialisation. The workforce was essentially illiterate, unskilled and undisciplined. The main problems facing managers in factories were drunkenness and absenteeism – many workers returned to their villages after they had failed to come to terms with the discipline of factory life.

Between 1929 and 1937 investment in education and training schemes created a skilled workforce. A new **elite** emerged – teachers, scientists, engineers, factory managers and skilled workers who were paid far higher wages than ordinary workers.

Like many officials, they also received extra benefits, such as better housing or the right to buy scarce foods. They enjoyed a higher standard of living, which went against communist principles, but Stalin realised that incentives had to be used in order to attract the correct calibre of people.

Opportunities for women

Source D: **A female machinist in a tractor factory in Stalingrad in the 1930s**

Source E: Women going to work in a **collective farm**. Their babies are being looked after in the crèche while they work

Women were encouraged to work to help achieve the plans. Facilities such as crèches were provided to help them continue working after childbirth (see Source E). There were some improvements in education and health for the workers and their families. All workers' children received free primary education and free healthcare schemes were extended to cover most of the workforce.

Over-ambitious targets

The targets of the Five-Year Plans were frequently too ambitious and set at unrealistic levels. As a result, some were not achieved. Officials at every level often gave false or exaggerated production figures in order to satisfy the demands of *Gosplan*. The production of textiles actually declined during the first Five-Year Plan and the housing industry was virtually ignored. Above all, there was a serious shortage of consumer goods.

Quality remained an over-riding problem in each of the plans. Many of the workers were peasants, with little experience of working with machines, for example, half of the tractors produced for the collective farms soon broke down. Industry grew so rapidly that the shortage of skilled workers became a real problem, so much so that the first Five-Year Plan produced only 50,000 tractors when the target was 170,000.

Tasks

5. *Why do you think that Stalin focused on eradicating illiteracy in the 1930s?*

6. *Can you suggest any disadvantages for Stalin if he had a literate workforce?*

7. *Study Sources C, D and E. Why do you think that many of the propaganda photographs about agricultural and industrial change featured women?*

Working and living conditions

Economic progress was often achieved at the expense of harsh living and working conditions. Some of the biggest tasks in the Plans were carried out in appalling conditions by forced labour – prisoners in *gulags*. Many of these workers were peasants who had opposed collectivisation (see pages 106–108) and they built, amongst other projects, the Belomor Canal and the Moscow Metro. These conditions are described by an eyewitness in Source F.

Peasants were also pressed into working in the factories. They were not used to the harsh industrial regime and experienced terrible conditions, similar to the workers before the Revolution. Millions died as a result of Stalin's policies and yet there were people who defended the vision Stalin put forward; that his policies meant a strong Soviet Union.

Source F: **An eyewitness account of conditions during the building of the Belomor Canal in the 1930s**

At the end of the day there were corpses left on the worksite. Two were frozen back to back leaning against each other. At night sledges went out and collected them. In the summer, bones remained from corpses which had not been removed in time.

It proved impossible to build enough new houses for the millions of peasants who flooded into the cities or worked in the new industrial centres. Most families had to live in overcrowded and run-down buildings, such as those described in Source H.

Source H: **A description of a Moscow apartment by Freda Utley, from her memoirs** *Lost Illusion*, **1949. Utley was an American Marxist who lived in the Soviet Union during the 1930s**

Badly built, with doors and windows of unseasoned wood, which could not be shut properly. Unpapered and thinly whitewashed walls, these two rooms were home. By American and British standards, we were living in a squalid tenement house. But by Soviet Russian standards we were housed almost as Communist aristocrats. We not only had two rooms to live in. We had the luxury of gas for cooking. Best of all we had a bathroom with a lavatory, which we had to share with only one other family.

Workers were poorly paid. The value of their wages fell by 50 per cent, meaning that something they could buy in 1928 cost them twice as much in 1933. There was a great shortage of everyday goods, and there were few workmen to carry out domestic repairs. Crime, alcoholism and juvenile delinquency increased.

Source G: **Photograph showing working conditions on the Belomor Canal**

Fines were imposed for lateness and bad workmanship and workers who were absent for more than a day were sacked. Failures were always blamed on **saboteurs** rather than on the system. The secret police encouraged workers to inform on one another. Anyone blamed for obstructing work could be sent to a labour camp or shot. In 1928, 55 engineers working in the Shakhty coal-mines in the Donbass were accused of sabotaging equipment and organising accidents and were put on trial. Despite their innocence, five were shot.

Source I: Khrushchev, in a speech made in 1956, after Stalin's death, about the effects of industrialisation. He was talking about how people just 'disappeared' in the 1930s

Both these managers perished in 1937. They disappeared off the face of the earth without leaving so much as a trace. Nobody could tell what happened to them. I don't know how many factory managers and engineers perished in this way. It was easy to get rid of someone you didn't like. All you had to do was submit a report denouncing him as an enemy of the people. The local party organisation would glance at your report and have the man taken care of.

Tasks

8. *What can you learn from Source I about the effects of industrialisation?*

9a. *Make your own balance sheet showing the successes and failures of industrialisation. Set it out as a two-column table as in the example below.*

Successes	Failures

b. *Overall, do you think the successes outweigh the failures? Give reasons for your answer.*

10. *If living and working conditions were harsh, why were there so few strikes or demonstrations against them? (Look back to pages 100–103 to help you with this answer.)*

Examination practice

Question 1 – 'In what ways . . .'
In what ways did the Five-Year Plans change the life of the Soviet worker? (7 marks)

How to answer
There are often questions in Section (a) of Paper 1 which begin – 'In what ways did . . .?' Such a question should be straightforward:
- Check to see how many marks are to be awarded – normally five or seven – and then begin to plan your answer.
- Jot down key points and make sure you can organise them into their order of importance.
- This question is worth seven marks so you need to explain at least three changes.
- The question is about change – ensure that you look at changes. Often students will write about the causes and then move into changes – this only wastes time and there is no reward for this approach.
- Begin the answer with the actual words of the question – this will ensure that the focus is clear and sharp.

Why did Stalin decide on collectivisation?

Source A: A propaganda photograph of 1931 showing Russian peasants enthusiastically queuing up to join a collective. The photograph was used across the Soviet Union and was entitled 'We would like to work together'

As with the Five-Year Plans, Stalin had a mixture of economic and political motives behind the decision to change Soviet agriculture.

Stalin decided to collectivise the farms after food shortages in 1927 and 1928. Collectivisation meant that peasants had to give up their small plots of land and animals and pool them with those of other families in order to make a farm large enough to use machinery and modern farming methods.

Collectivisation was supposed to be undertaken on a voluntary basis, but within a year it was being imposed on the peasants. Anyone who opposed the process was labelled as a *kulak* and an enemy of the state and deported to Siberia and the Urals.

Local party officials went into villages and explained how the collective farm or *kolkhoz* would

Kulak
The name given to the better-off peasants who had benefited from Lenin's New Economic Policy. From selling their produce, these peasants became more well-off than other peasants and began to employ poorer peasants to work for them.

be organised. The most important figure was the chairman, who was a Bolshevik Party member, usually from the towns. The collective farm replaced the mir or village commune. The collective would then claim ownership of animals, grain supplies and buildings in the village.

Kolkhoz

By 1940, there were about 240,000 *kolkhoz*. They were normally made up of 80 or so peasant families who farmed around 500 hectares of land. The families had to provide a fixed amount of food for the state at very low prices and peasants received a small wage. The peasant could keep any surplus.

The state provided each collective farm with machinery, especially a tractor, other tools and seeds. In addition, Motor Tractor Stations (MTS) were set up. There was normally one of these for every 40 collective farms. Tractors and drivers from the MTS moved between the collectives to carry out the ploughing.

Sovkhoz

There was also a type of farm called a *sovkhoz* – here, all land was owned by the state and the peasants worked as paid labourers. All produce was taken by the state.

Reasons for collectivisation

Industrialisation was to be supported by food surpluses created by changes in agricultural production. Stalin knew that the West would not loan the Soviet Union money, nor could he expect any investment from foreign countries. The agricultural surpluses would therefore finance the initial stages of the Five-Year Plans. The produce would be sold abroad and the foreign exchange would pay for machinery and overseas technicians.

As well as wanting to modernise the Soviet Union, Stalin also sought to control the people – this time the peasants – through collectivisation.

The grain crisis of 1927

Before collectivisation, Soviet peasants used old-fashioned, inefficient farming methods. Agriculture was still based on small peasant plots with little use of machinery. Even under the New Economic Policy (see pages 72–73), farmers were not producing enough food for the workers in the cities. After 1926, the amount of surplus grain given to the government by the peasants had been falling. The peasants had become wary of growing too much food, knowing it would be seized by the state at a low price. There was said to be a 'grain crisis' in 1927 and Stalin was keen to ensure adequate supplies.

The needs of industrialisation

If the Five-Year Plans were to be successful, agriculture had to be modernised. Mechanisation was the key, because it would release large numbers of peasants to work in the towns and cities. Fewer peasants, therefore, would have to produce more food, as even greater numbers of workers would have to be fed. Stalin had created a problem for himself. He needed workers to create machinery for industry and agriculture but, to do this, peasants would have to move into towns. Yet, this would reduce the number of workers on the land and he needed agricultural production to increase in order to sell food abroad to bring in foreign currency to allow him to invest in materials for his factories. It was an insoluble problem – unless some sections were to starve.

Destroy the kulaks

Stalin also had political reasons. He disliked the richer peasants – the *kulaks* – who, in the eyes of the communists, hoarded food for their own consumption, rather than providing it for industrial workers in the towns. This is clearly shown in Sources B and C (page 108).

There was increasing pressure on the government to remove this capitalist class. However, the majority of the peasants were not *kulaks* and any changes to the farming system – especially collectivisation – would be met by opposition from a large number of them. Most peasants were by nature conservative in their outlook, and they had already shown in the civil war and the 1920s that they were not completely convinced by the theories of the Bolsheviks.

> **Source B: Extracts from speeches made about collectivisation by Stalin in 1928 and 1929**
>
> *Look at the kulak farms: their barns and sheds are crammed with grain. They are waiting for prices to rise. So long as there are kulaks there will be sabotage of our grain needs. The effect will be that our towns and industrial centres, as well as the **Red Army**, will be threatened with hunger. We cannot allow that. We must break the resistance of this class and deprive it of its existence.*

Source C: From a speech by Stalin to the Communist Party of the Soviet Union in 1929. Here he was threatening the *kulaks*

We must eliminate the kulaks as a class. We must smash the kulaks . . . we must strike at the kulaks so hard as to prevent them from rising to their feet again. We must annihilate them as a social class.

Communist ideals

Collectivisation fitted in with communist ideas of common ownership. In 1925, as a result of the New Economic Policy (see pages 72–73), less than one per cent of the land was collectivised. Moreover, the policy would also enable Stalin to strengthen his dictatorship. He would be able to discredit the Right, led by Bukharin, who supported the New Economic Policy and opposed collectivisation.

Control of the countryside

In addition, it would give Stalin control over the countryside and the peasantry, something that Lenin had failed to achieve. Stalin did not trust the peasants. He saw them as natural enemies of communism and he was aware of how close they had come to destroying Lenin during the time of War Communism (see pages 68–70). He believed that by taking away the peasants' independence, gained as a result of their ownership of the land, he could remove any threat from them once and for all.

Tasks

1. *Look at all Stalin's motives for collectivisation and put them in a rank order of importance, beginning with the one you think is the most important at the top. Give a brief explanation for each choice you make. If you work in small groups, you can compare lists and see if there is any agreement.*

2. *How effective do you think the propaganda photograph, Source D, would be in turning the Soviet people against the kulaks? Give reasons for your answer.*

3. *Study Sources B (see page 107) and C. Explain why Stalin was keen to focus on the kulaks as enemies of the state.*

Source D: Peasants protesting against the *kulaks*

What opposition was there to collectivisation?

There was fierce opposition to collectivisation, especially in the agricultural areas of the Ukraine and Caucasus. Many peasants set fire to their farms and slaughtered their animals, rather than hand them over to the state. The scale of the slaughter was staggering – from a total of 60 million cows, 30 million were killed, and 16 million horses died from a total of 34 million. This is clearly explained in Source A.

Source A: From *Virgin Soil Upturned*, a novel by M. Sholokov, 1934. Sholokov lived in the Soviet Union during the period of collectivisation

Both those who had joined the kolkhoz *and individual farmers killed their stock. Bulls, sheep, pigs and even cows were slaughtered. The dogs began to drag entrails around the village; cellars and barns were full of meat. Young and old suffered from stomach ache. At dinner times tables groaned under boiled and roasted meat.*

De-kulakisation

Stalin retaliated by sending in de-kulakisation squads – Party members from the towns and the **OGPU** – to round up opponents of his policy as explained in Source B. It is impossible to find an accurate figure, but possibly as many as ten million people were deported in the war against the *kulaks.*

The extent of opposition forced Stalin to slow down the process of collectivisation in 1930. Indeed, he blamed over-keen party officials for the problems in carrying out his policy and, during the spring and summer of that year, there was some reversal of the process. He also made some concessions, including allowing members of the collectives to have some animals and a small garden plot for their own use. However, in late 1930, collectivisation began again and, by 1932, 62 per cent of peasant households had been collectivised, and five years later the number had increased to 93 per cent.

Source B: From Victor Kravchenko's book *I Chose Freedom*. He witnessed collectivisation and the attack on the *kulaks* in one village. Kravchenko was a high-ranking Soviet official in the 1930s who eventually sought political asylum in the USA

A number of women were weeping hysterically and calling the name of their fathers and husbands. In the background, guarded by the OGPU and soldiers with drawn revolvers, stood about twenty peasants, young and old, with bundles on their backs. A few were weeping. The others stood there sad and helpless. So this was 'liquidation of the kulaks *as a class'. A lot of simple peasants being torn from their native soil, stripped of all their worldly goods and shipped to some distant labour camps.*

Tasks

1. *Describe the key features of collectivisation.*

(Remember how to answer this type of question? For further guidance see page 99.)

2. *What were the immediate effects of collectivisation?*

3. *Study Source B. What can you learn from this source about the* kulaks *and collectivisation?*

4. *Explain why you think that the* kulaks *were so opposed to collectivisation.*

What were the effects of collectivisation?

1 Human cost

The human cost of collectivisation was enormous. There was a serious famine from 1932–33, which caused the death of somewhere between six and ten million peasants.

Source A: Photograph of victims of the famine during the first phase of collectivisation circa 1931

2 Benefits

The aim of producing enough food to feed the towns and the Red Army was achieved. Life on the collective farms was not all bad. For example, there were schools and hospitals on some collectives for the workers. The MTS (see page 107) were quite successful and the mechanisation of farming did speed up in the years after 1935. By 1936, more than 90 per cent of land had been collectivised and tractors were introduced on a large scale.

Effects of collectivisation

3 Fall in production

Economically, collectivisation had mixed results. Peasant opposition led to a serious decline in grain production, from 73.3 million tonnes in 1928 to 67.6 million in 1934. The impact on the countryside was worsened by the government policy of seizing grain. The rural population starved in order to provide for the needs of industry and peasants moved to the towns in search of food. Such movement was stopped when the government introduced passports simply for moving around the Soviet Union. Consequently, the peasants became tied to the collectives and were in little better position than the **serfs** of tsarist Russia.

Source B: The figures below are Western estimates based on Soviet statistics

Consumption of foodstuffs (in kilos per head)				
	Bread	Potatoes	Meat	Lard/Butter
1928	250.4	141.1	24.8	1.35
1932	214.6	125.0	11.2	0.7
Comparative numbers of livestock				
	Horses	Cattle	Pigs	Sheep & Goats
1928	33,000,000	70,000,000	26,000,000	146,000,000
1932	15,000,000	34,000,000	9,000,000	42,000,000

4 Inefficient farming

Farming remained inefficient with Soviet farmers producing less per head than farmers in the USA or Western Europe. Until the mid-1930s, there was not enough food grown for the whole Soviet population and some had to be bought from abroad. The worst years were 1932–33 when a national famine occurred. In the Ukraine and the northern Caucasus about five million people died. It was not until 1940 that figures for grain production matched those of 1914. Historians have found little evidence that collectivisation provided surplus to sell abroad and this failed to provide adequate foreign capital for Stalin's investment programme.

Source C: Soviet cartoon of a peasant working on his own plot of land rather than in the collective

5 Greater control

Collectivisation was also a success for Stalin and the communists. They had finally secured control of the countryside. The peasants never again openly rebelled against communist rule. Stalin had also ensured that he had a secure supply of food for the towns and workers for the factories.

Source D: From a report by a government official in 1933. He was writing about collectivisation

It took a famine to show the peasants who was master.

Tasks

1. What can you learn from Source A about the effects of collectivisation?

(Remember how to answer this type of question? For further guidance see page 16.)

2a. Look at the effects of collectivisation. Organise the effects into successes and failures and set out your answer as a two-column table as below.

Successes	Failures

b. Overall, do you think the successes outweigh the failures?

3. Study Source B.

a. What can you learn from the source about the impact of collectivisation on food production?

b. Why do think that the provenance of the source says 'Western estimates based on Soviet statistics'?

Were Stalin's economic policies a success?

Economically and politically, Stalin's policies were a success in the long term. Collectivisation and the Five-Year Plans dragged the Soviet economy into the twentieth century. The economy was able to withstand the German invasion in 1941 and sustain four years of war. Politically, Stalin had secured firm control of industry and agriculture, and his idea of 'socialism in one country' was now firmly established in urban and rural areas.

Socially, however, at what expense had his policies been imposed? Harsh living and working conditions in the towns, the wholesale use of slave labour, famine and the elimination of a class of people had created chaos in the country. Did the end justify the means?

Source A: Table showing increase in arms expenditure during the Five-Year Plans			
	1933	**1937**	**1940**
Total spent by the government (in millions of roubles)	42,080	106,238	174,350
Defence spending (in millions of roubles)	1,421	17,481	56,800
Defence spending as a % of total government expenditure	3.4%	16.5%	32.6%

Soviet poster published in 1935. It shows Stalin and Marshal Voroshilov, head of the armed forces. The caption was 'Long live the Red Workers' and Peasants' Army, Loyal Guardians of the Soviet Frontiers'.

Tasks

1. Study Source A. What can you learn about Stalin's overall aim during the Five-Year Plans?

2. Hold a class debate to discuss Stalin as leader of the Soviet Union. The title of the debate is:

'Stalin's methods were justified because without him, there would have been no strong Soviet Union by 1941.'

The Soviet Union, 1941–53

9

Tasks

1. *What are the cartoonist's views of the Pact?*

2. *How does he get his views across?*

Source A: A British cartoon of 1939 about the Nazi-Soviet Pact of the same year. Hitler is shown on the left and Stalin on the right

In 1941, Nazi Germany invaded the Soviet Union. Although Stalin had expected this, the Soviet Union was not prepared. Nevertheless, both the Soviet Union and Stalin survived and played their part in the eventual defeat of Germany. In the years that followed the Second World War, Stalin continued his purges but expanded Soviet influence into Eastern Europe, sparking off the Cold War with the USA and Western Europe.

This chapter will examine the following questions:

• Why did the Soviet Union survive the German invasion of 1941?
• What effects did the war have?
• Why did the Cold War begin?
• What were the key features of the period 1945–53?
• What problems Stalin did leave?

Exam skills

Advice is given on how to answer causation questions (ii) and (iii) in Section (a) of Paper 1. These are worth 5 marks and often ask the causes and consequences of important events.

Why did the Soviet Union survive the German invasion of 1941?

The German invasion of 1941 was, at first, very successful, with massive German advances. However, the Battle of Stalingrad during the winter of 1942–43 was to be a major turning point in the war.

Why did Nazi Germany invade?

In 1939, Stalin signed a non-aggression pact with Nazi Germany, in which the Soviet Union agreed to remain neutral when Hitler, the German dictator, invaded Poland. In return, the Soviet Union was allowed to occupy eastern Poland. Within two years of the agreement, German armies were invading the Soviet Union.

Hitler had long made it clear that he intended to invade the USSR. He wanted to destroy communism and turn Russia into a German colony. Nevertheless the invasion, when it came in June 1941, took Stalin by surprise.

What impact did the invasion have?

The attack came in June 1941, when three powerful German armies drove deep into the Soviet Union at a rate of 70 kilometres a day. The German airforce destroyed most of the Soviet planes on the ground. By the end of October 1941, German troops had destroyed 20,000 Soviet tanks and taken over two million prisoners. In the south they had captured Kiev and further north were closing in on Leningrad and Moscow.

This early German success was due to Stalin's lack of preparation and the impact of the purges in which he had removed most of the commanders of the armed forces, leaving a very inexperienced leadership.

How did the Soviet Union survive?

The German attack was halted at the end of 1941 outside Moscow and Leningrad. This was due to the heroic resistance of the Soviets, but mainly as a

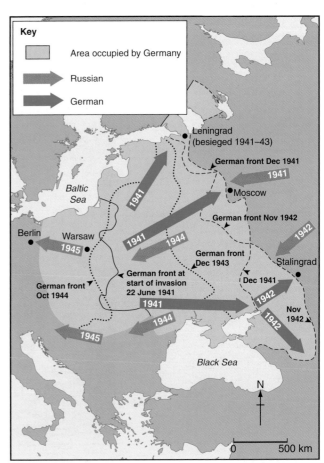

Map showing the key events on the Eastern Front, 1941–45

result of the extreme winter weather. The Germans attacked again in 1942, but at the end of the year were defeated at the Battle of Stalingrad, one of the turning points of the war. From 1943 onwards, the Red Army gradually forced the Germans back into their own country. Soviet troops entered Berlin in the spring of 1945.

The Soviet weather

Soviet survival and eventual success was due to a variety of reasons. Firstly, the extreme Soviet weather during the winter of 1941–42 severely handicapped the German advance. It began to pour with rain in October 1941. This slowed down the German advance as roads turned into rivers of mud. This was followed, in November, by record-breaking temperatures, as low as -35 degrees C. Without anti-freeze, German vehicle radiators froze and German soldiers were ill-equipped to cope with such extremes of cold.

Stalin's leadership

Stalin quickly recovered his nerve after the initial German attack. He began a policy of all out war against the Germans. For example, he introduced a 'scorched earth' policy, insisting on the destruction of anything in the path of the German armies, including crops and factories, for instance. This deprived the advancing German armies of much needed supplies. He replaced useless army leaders like Voroshilov with more able men such as Zhukov. He used every means to inspire his people. He appealed to them to fight for 'Mother Russia' rather than communism.

Source A: **A Soviet painting, 1948, which shows Stalin personally planning the defeat of the German armies**

The heroism of the Soviet people

Many Russians, in areas occupied by the Germans, became **partisans** and showed considerable

Source B: **An extract from a Soviet textbook published in 1976**

Zina Portnova was a young Pioneer. Zina became a partisan. One day, when on an assignment, she was captured. The officer questioning brandished a pistol at her and then put it back in his desk. She grabbed it and shot the officer dead. With a second shot she killed another officer and . . .

courage. They ambushed and murdered Germans, acted as spies, and blew up bridges and railway lines in occupied territory.

The entire Soviet population was mobilised for war. Those men not in the army, women and children worked in the factories or helped to dig huge tank traps and other defences. By 1943, the Soviets were producing more war material than the Germans.

Hitler's mistakes

Hitler's mistakes also contributed greatly to Soviet success. The German invasion of 1941 was launched too late in the year to avoid the impact of the Russian winter. Hitler sacrificed many soldiers in trying to hold on to Stalingrad in the winter of 1942–43.

Tasks

1. Give one reason to explain why Hitler invaded the Soviet Union in 1941.

(Remember how to answer this type of question? For further guidance see page 81.)

2. Source B only tells part of the story about this Soviet partisan. What else did she do?

Either:

a. Write the next paragraph

b. Draw a storyboard to illustrate the rest of the story.

Remember that the account is to glorify the role of the partisans.

3. How useful are Sources A and B as evidence of the Soviet war effort?

(Remember how to answer this type of question? For further guidance see pages 37–39.)

What effects did the war have?

The Second World War brought great suffering, death and devastation to the USSR and yet it emerged along with the USA as a superpower.

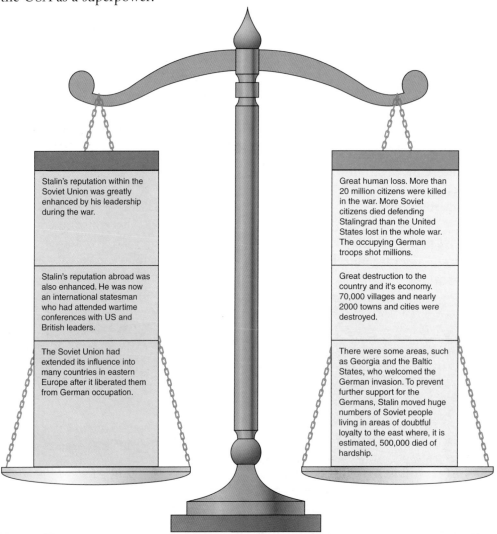

Stalin's reputation within the Soviet Union was greatly enhanced by his leadership during the war.

Stalin's reputation abroad was also enhanced. He was now an international statesman who had attended wartime conferences with US and British leaders.

The Soviet Union had extended its influence into many countries in eastern Europe after it liberated them from German occupation.

Great human loss. More than 20 million citizens were killed in the war. More Soviet citizens died defending Stalingrad than the United States lost in the whole war. The occupying German troops shot millions.

Great destruction to the country and it's economy. 70,000 villages and nearly 2000 towns and cities were destroyed.

There were some areas, such as Georgia and the Baltic States, who welcomed the German invasion. To prevent further support for the Germans, Stalin moved huge numbers of Soviet people living in areas of doubtful loyalty to the east where, it is estimated, 500,000 died of hardship.

Task

The scales above show some of the effects of the war on the Soviet Union. The scales are evenly balanced. Should they be, or should the gains outweigh the losses, or vice versa?
In groups:

- *First summarise each of the effects in a few words.*

- *Then put them on your own drawn set of scales. How should they be balanced – equally; with gains outweighing losses; or losses outweighing gains?*

- *Feedback to the rest of the class, giving reasons for your choice.*

Examination practice

Five-mark questions

In Section (a) of Paper 1 you will have to answer five-mark questions.

How to answer

For the five-mark question you need to write at least two good length paragraphs. You could plan your answer by following the steps below.

Now have a go yourself

1 Why did the Soviet Union survive the German invasion of 1941? (5 marks)

2 What effects did the Second World War have on the Soviet Union? (5 marks)

3 Describe the key features of the German invasion of the Soviet Union in 1941. (5 marks)

4 In what ways was Stalin able to strengthen his control of the Soviet Union during the Second World War? (5 marks)

(Remember how to answer question 3? For further guidance see pages 99 and 105.)

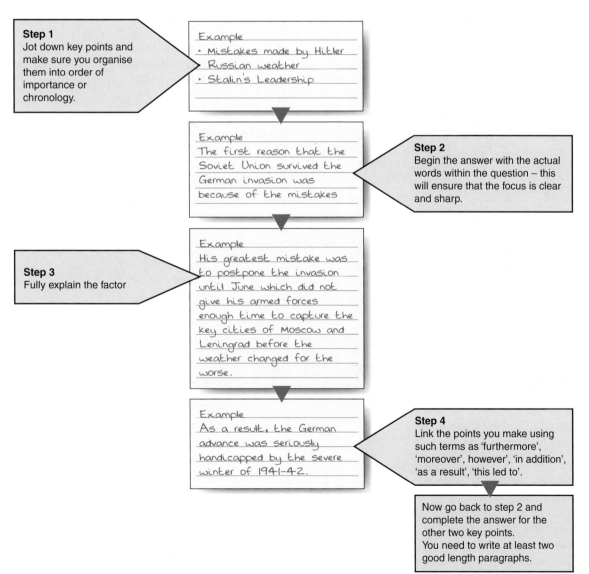

Step 1
Jot down key points and make sure you organise them into order of importance or chronology.

Example
· Mistakes made by Hitler
  Russian weather
· Stalin's Leadership

Example
The first reason that the Soviet Union survived the German invasion was because of the mistakes

Step 2
Begin the answer with the actual words within the question – this will ensure that the focus is clear and sharp.

Step 3
Fully explain the factor

Example
His greatest mistake was to postpone the invasion until June which did not give his armed forces enough time to capture the key cities of Moscow and Leningrad before the weather changed for the worse.

Example
As a result, the German advance was seriously handicapped by the severe winter of 1941-42.

Step 4
Link the points you make using such terms as 'furthermore', 'moreover', 'however', 'in addition', 'as a result', 'this led to'.

Now go back to step 2 and complete the answer for the other two key points.
You need to write at least two good length paragraphs.

Why did the Cold War begin?

Although allies during the Second World War, the USSR and the USA became more and more suspicious of each other in the years that followed Germany's defeat in 1945. Soon, a state of tension known as the 'Cold War' existed between them. Even before the war ended there had been tension between the USSR and the Western powers. Stalin was convinced that Britain and the USA had delayed the invasion of France until 1944 deliberately, in order to see the Soviet Union weakened by its struggle against Germany on the Eastern Front.

Once the war ended, Stalin was determined to ensure that the Soviet Union was well defended against future attack by creating **buffer states** in Eastern Europe between the Soviet Union and Germany. He took advantage of the fact that his army was already in occupation to take over Estonia, Lithuania, Latvia, Finland and parts of Poland. He took some territory from Germany, including Eastern Prussia. In addition he ensured, between 1945 and 1947, that communist governments were elected in Czechoslovakia, Hungary, Poland, Bulgaria and Romania. These became known as Soviet **satellite states**.

Britain and the USA were alarmed by this Soviet expansion. Rather than seeing it as Stalin's attempt to protect the Soviet Union against future invasion from the west, they believed he was deliberately trying to spread communism throughout Europe. As early as 1946, the former British Prime Minister, Winston Churchill, accused the Soviet Union of having drawn an 'Iron Curtain' across Europe – of separating east from west. Britain and the USA were determined to prevent further Soviet expansion into Western Europe.

Within ten years, the two sides had set up rival **alliance blocs**. In 1949, the North Atlantic Treaty Organisation (**NATO**) brought the United States and most of Western Europe together in a military alliance. Six years later, the Soviet Union set up its own alliance with the states in Eastern Europe known as the **Warsaw Pact**.

Soviet expansion, 1939–after 1945

Tasks

1. *Why did the Western powers and the Soviet Union become rivals in the years following the defeat of Germany in 1945?*

(Remember how to answer this type of question? For further guidance see page 81.)

2. *The Western powers and the Soviet Union each had totally different interpretations or views of the expansion of Soviet influence into Eastern Europe. Write a paragraph from two different history textbooks explaining this expansion:*

• *From a Soviet history textbook*

• *From a British or American history textbook.*

The Russian Revolution and Soviet Union 1910–91

What were the key features of the period 1945–53?

Source A: Ilya Ehrenburg, a Russian, remembers in 1965 how optimistic she was about the future of Russia after the war

I firmly believed that after victory everything would suddenly change. Everybody expected that once victory had been won, people would know real happiness. We realised, of course, that the country had been devastated, impoverished and that we would have to work hard. We did not have fantasies about mountains of gold. But we believed that victory would bring justice, that human dignity would triumph.

Victory in the Second World War seemed to strengthen Stalin's position and yet he kept up his purges and harsh policies. He continued to persecute those who he believed had collaborated with the Germans, especially those who had allowed themselves to be captured alive and made prisoners of war. He deported entire ethnic groups, such as the Crimean Tatars, to Central Asia and Kazakhstan.

Anyone who dared to question Stalin's policies was purged – most notably poets, artists, scientists and musicians. There was also a systematic persecution of Jews. Rumours of further purges spread in the early 1950s. Nobody was safe, not even Georgi Malenkov, who was being groomed as Stalin's successor. Stalin's suspicions of the West led him to demand still greater attention to state security and the elimination of any potential rivals. 'Enemy elements' were rounded up and sent to labour camps. Any signs of Western influence were condemned and severely dealt with.

He continued to fear plots against him. He transferred high-ranking officers like Marshall Zhukov to less important posts and increased the Communist Party's control over the army. He promoted younger men like Leonid Brezhnev to weaken the power of other leading communists, such as Molotov, Beria and Khrushchev. In 1952, the state press published details of the 'Doctors' Plot'. This was an entirely imaginary account of an attempt by Jewish doctors to murder Stalin.

The Five-Year Plans also continued after the war. The fourth Five-Year Plan (1946–50) aimed to restore the economy to pre-war levels. The results were impressive. Industrial production recovered quickly, helped by the work of over two million slave labourers.

The fifth Five-Year Plan was less successful. Large amounts of resources were diverted to ambitious building projects, which had little practical value at a time when there were serious shortages of houses. There were still severe punishments for being late, absent or caught drunk at work.

On 2 March 1953, Stalin suffered a brain haemorrhage. His personal doctor, Professor Vinogradov, was not there to treat him because he had been arrested the previous year for suggesting that Stalin should take things easily. Lavrenti Beria, the head of the NKVD, was sent for. He was found in a government villa with a woman and arrived very drunk at 3 a.m. Stalin was left untreated and died on 5 March.

Source B: A poster of 1948, which says 'Carry out the Five-Year Plan in Four Years'

Task

Study Source A. Was Ilya Ehrenburg right to be optimistic? Explain your answer.

What problems did Stalin leave?

Stalin lying in state to encourage the 'Cult of Stalin' after his death. Indeed, many Soviet citizens genuinely grieved his death.

Stalin had turned the Soviet Union into a superpower but left behind a number of problems.

The Soviet Union was now involved in a Cold War with the West, which meant huge amounts of money had to be spent on arms development and maintaining control of the satellite states in Eastern Europe.

Although Stalin's industrial achievements seemed impressive, collectivisation had not solved the food shortages. Central control of economic planning destroyed local initiatives to sort out problems in industry. Local managers lied about production quotas for fear of being punished. There was far too much emphasis on heavy industrial goods such as metals, electricity and chemicals. Consumer goods continued to be neglected.

There were serious shortages in housing. In the Ukraine, Belorussia and much of the European part of Russia alone, 25 million people lost their homes in the war.

Strict censorship meant that people were still only supposed to enjoy books, art and music that followed 'Socialist Realism' (see page 83).

Tasks

1. Describe the key features of Stalin's rule in the years 1945–53.

(Remember how to answer this type of question? For further guidance see page 99.)

2. You are a British journalist living in Moscow when Stalin died. Your newspaper editor has asked you to write an obituary of Stalin. An obituary is a public announcement of a famous person's death, together with a brief biography including key achievements.

a. Begin by doing your own balance sheet of his successes and failures.

Successes	Failures

b. Now write your obituary in no more than 150 words. It must cover both his successes and failures.

Khrushchev and the Soviet Union

Source A

From the memoirs of Yevgeny Yevtushenko, a Soviet poet. He was writing about the funeral of Stalin

I'll never forget going to see Stalin's coffin. The crowd turned into a monstrous whirlpool. I was walking but was carried along by the crowd. I was saved by my height. Smaller people were smothered alive. People howled – 'Get the trucks out of the way!'

'I can't – I've got no instructions,' a very young, bewildered police officer shouted back from one of the trucks.

All at once I felt a savage hatred for everything that had given birth to that 'No instructions', shouted when people were dying because of someone's stupidity.

For the first time in my life I thought with hatred of the man we were burying. He could not be innocent of the disaster.

Task

What can you learn from Source A about Stalin's rule in the Soviet Union?

This chapter examines the policies of Khrushchev as leader of the Soviet Union after the death of Stalin. It will answer the following questions:

• Why did Khrushchev emerge as leader?
• Why was de-Stalinisation introduced?
• What changes were made to industry?
• What changes were made to agriculture?
• Why did Khrushchev fall from power?

Exam skills

This chapter gives you guidance on the ten-mark question in Section (b) of Paper 1. This could either be a causation, consequence or change essay or a two-part question in which you choose two items to explain.

Why did Khrushchev emerge as leader?

> **Source A:** From *Bolshevism and Stalinism* by S. Cohen, written in 1980. Here the author is assessing Stalin's rule
>
> *Stalinism was excess, extraordinary extremism . . . a Holocaust by terror that victimised tens of millions of people. It was not merely a leader cult but the deification of a despot . . .*

On the death of Stalin in 1953, Georgi Malenkov became Prime Minister and Nikita Khrushchev became Party Secretary. These two and another two – Bulganin and Molotov – ruled the Soviet Union by committee. They called their approach 'collective leadership'. These senior members of the Communist Party were against the idea of one man dominating the Soviet Union.

Each was wary of the Head of the Secret Police, Lavrenti Beria, and they plotted to remove him, having him executed in December 1953. Among the leading group, it was thought that Malenkov would emerge as the eventual leader of the Soviet Union.

Khrushchev was not an intellectual but his experiences in the Party and the war had made him a ruthless politician. He was not seen as a potential leader – his humble background and lack of education worked against him. However, his colleagues underestimated his ambition and failed to see his ruthlessness.

The 'New Course'

Malenkov put forward the 'New Course' to:

- improve living standards
- increase the production of consumer goods
- expand light industry
- increase food production
- relax Stalin's terror system.

However, his promises could not be fulfilled and not enough consumer goods were produced, which enabled criticism to be levelled against him. Furthermore, there were criticisms within the leadership about his failure to concentrate on heavy industry. Khrushchev also disagreed about Malenkov's agricultural policy and suggested using large areas of unused land.

Malenkov sought to reduce tension with the West and had plans to reduce defence expenditure. This did not endear him to Soviet generals.

Task

1. *Look at Sources A and B and the information above. Explain why after Stalin's death, the main figures of the Communist Party established a 'collective leadership'.*

Source B: Soviet leaders at Stalin's funeral, 1953. Left to right – Khrushchev, Beria, Malenkov, Bulganin, Voroshilov and Kaganovich

Khrushchev becomes dominant

Khrushchev increased his standing in the Soviet Union by travelling around the country and making contact with a broad range of officials. Moreover, as Party Secretary he was able to place his own followers in posts of authority, very much as Stalin had done. The army also supported Khrushchev, and Marshal Zhukov, Commander-in-Chief, had great admiration for a politician who had actually fought in the **Great Patriotic War**.

By 1955, Khrushchev had become the dominant member of the collective leadership and he felt able to attack Malenkov's policies as deviating from those of the Communist Party. Malenkov resigned and was replaced by Bulganin – it appeared that Khrushchev and Bulganin exercised shared power, but in effect Khrushchev was very much the senior partner.

There was an attempt to oust Khrushchev in 1957, when members of the *Politburo* tried to out-vote him. Khrushchev's position as Party Secretary meant that he was able to use Party members to block the *Politburo* by a vote of the Party. His opponents were labelled as 'the anti-Party group' and within twelve months, Bulganin, Molotov and Marshal Zhukov were removed from office and given positions well away from Moscow. Clearly, the political climate had changed – in Stalin's time, these people would have been executed.

Biography Nikita Khrushchev 1894–1971

1894 Born, son of a coal miner
1918 Joined the Bolshevik Party
1918–20 Served as a Commissar in the Red Army
1931 Communist Party of the Soviet Union (CPSU) District Secretary in Moscow
1938 Chief of the Communist Party in the Ukraine
1939 Appointed to the *Politburo*
1942 Fought at Stalingrad
1949 Head of CPSU in Moscow
1953 Appointed Communist Party Secretary
1958 Appointed Prime Minister
1959 Visited the USA
1962 Involved in the **Cuban Missiles Crisis**
1964 Removed from office
1971 Died in Moscow

Tasks

2. Describe the key features of the 'New Course'.

(Remember how to answer this type of question? For further guidance see page 99.)

3. With a partner list the main reasons why Khrushchev was able to emerge as sole leader of the Soviet Union.

Why was de-Stalinisation introduced?

Source A: From Khrushchev's speech to the Twentieth Congress in February 1956

Stalin abused his power, brutally violated Lenin's ideas and indulged in administrative violence, mass repression and terror ... with monstrously falsified lies he killed thousands of communists ... and ordered mass deportations of whole peoples ... He was capricious, irritable and brutal ... His rule was one of torture and oppression.

Task

Read Source A. Why do you think Khrushchev was careful to focus on Stalin's character?

There were some indications after 1953 that Stalin's record might be re-examined – the 'New Course' was testimony to this. However, the events at the Twentieth Congress took the politicians and people of the Soviet Union by complete surprise.

Khrushchev addressed the Twentieth Congress of the Soviet Communist Party on 24 February 1956. In the early stages of the Congress, he put forward a variety of proposals, which indicated that it would become policy to seek peaceful co-existence with the West and to increase production of consumer goods for Soviet citizens.

However, in a session that excluded the press, he attacked Stalin in what became known as the 'secret speech'. The speech took a weekend to deliver and, in it, Stalin's crimes and mistakes were clearly explained. Khrushchev read out Lenin's will which criticised Stalin, he ridiculed the idea of Stalin as a war hero, and said all the mistakes in the Soviet Union since 1934 had been a result of his 'mania for greatness'. His cult of personality was denounced.

Khrushchev was careful not to criticise the Communist Party, because this was the source of his own power. He ensured that blame for the wrongs of the past fell on Stalin's shoulders. Thus began the period of **de-Stalinisation**.

Within two years of the speech, about eight million political prisoners had been released from the feared *gulags* and those who had been killed under Stalin's rule were now declared innocent. There were many changes within the Soviet Union as the diagram below shows.

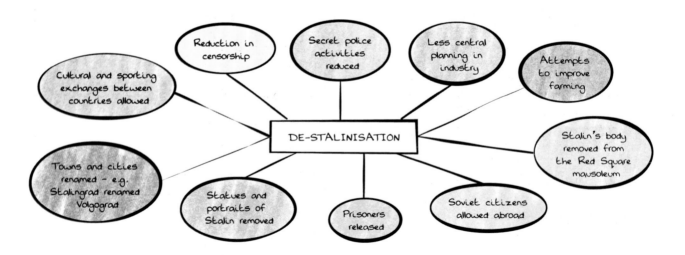

For Khrushchev, there were three key reasons for de-Stalinisation:

i) To distance himself from involvement in the work of Stalin – if Stalin were blamed for all the mistakes, then his links with him would be overlooked.

ii) To make the introduction of peaceful co-existence with other countries.

iii) To introduce drastic economic changes – there were not enough consumer goods and agriculture was still extremely inefficient. Stalin's methods had been wrong and Khrushchev could now introduce his 'Reform Communism', which would not only bring change but humanise the Soviet system.

Examination practice

The ten-mark essay question which appears in Section (b) of Paper 1 is often a causation or consequence question.
- Causation: why something happened.
- Consequence: the effects of an event.

Question 1 – ten-mark essay

What were the effects of de-Stalinisation on the Soviet Union? (10 marks)

How to answer

- This question is worth ten marks so there must be a well-developed answer, which explains three or four factors.
- Question 1, above, is a consequence question, so therefore three or four effects must be explained.
- The answer should begin with an introduction explaining any key terms in the question, e.g. de-Stalinisation, and giving the main effects that will be explained. See the example of an introduction above right.
- Each paragraph should begin with an effect which is then fully explained as precisely as possible.
- There should be an attempt to make links between some or all of the effects. Examiners look for suitable linking words, such as – as a result of, moreover, this led to, consequently, therefore, furthermore.
- To reach the top level of marks, there should be a conclusion which sums up the consequences and a judgement on the relative importance of the effects.

Example introduction

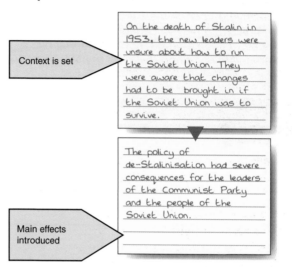

Context is set

> On the death of Stalin in 1953, the new leaders were unsure about how to run the Soviet Union. They were aware that changes had to be brought in if the Soviet Union was to survive.

Main effects introduced

> The policy of de-Stalinisation had severe consequences for the leaders of the Communist Party and the people of the Soviet Union.

Now complete the answer to question 1. Always plan your answer before writing it. Make a copy of the following planning grid to help you.

Introduction (see above)

First paragraph

Link e.g. *Moreover*

Second paragraph

Link e.g. *As a result*

Third paragraph

Link e.g. *Therefore*

Fourth paragraph

Conclusion e.g. *Overall*

Question 2 – ten-mark essay

Now have a go yourself

Why was the policy of de-Stalinisation followed after 1956? (10 marks)

What changes were made to industry?

Source A: From a Speech by Khrushchev in the late 1950s

We must help people to eat well, dress well and live well. You cannot put theory into your soup or Marxism into your clothes. If after forty years of Communism, a person cannot have a glass of milk or a pair of shoes, he will not believe that Communism is a good thing, no matter what you tell him.

Task

1. What can you learn from Source A about communism in the Soviet Union in the 1950s?

New economic plans

Stalin had stifled initiative and held back economic progress; there had to be different approaches and Khrushchev was prepared to move the Soviet Union forward.

In the years immediately after the death of Stalin, Malenkov announced targets to replace those of Stalin's fifth Five-Year Plan. The new targets placed emphasis on consumer goods, such as clothes, shoes, bicycles and watches. As ever, the targets were very ambitious and were only achieved in a few areas, such as the manufacture of motor cycles. A sixth Five-Year Plan was announced in 1956, only to be replaced by a Seven-Year Plan, which ran from 1959–65. This plan also emphasised consumer goods, as well as calling for growth in chemical industries to provide artificial fertilisers for agriculture.

Regional Economic Councils

The major change came in 1957 when Khrushchev announced a great scheme of administrative reform. Many (about 60) of the large and inefficient ministries in Moscow were closed down and more than 100 Regional Economic Councils

(*sovnarkhozy*) were set up to run the economy at a local level. Khrushchev was able to take power away from some of his opponents by these means, but this also brought another level of muddle to Russia's already complex system of economic planning. By 1960, Khrushchev realised that the system was not working. He tried to improve it by reducing the number of *sovnarkhozy* and by appointing committees of officials to supervise their work.

The result was that no one knew who was in charge, or what was expected of them. Though some of the targets in the Seven-Year Plan were achieved, rates of growth in industry remained low. Money had been diverted to finance armaments and space research and, as a result, other sectors of the economy began to lag behind.

Living standards

Despite the changes, the standard of living for the average Soviet citizen was much lower than that of the average person living in the West. Khrushchev planned fifteen million new dwellings to solve the housing shortage – factories were to make pre-fabricated flats – but the scheme was not successful. Nevertheless, between 1959 and 1965, about 50 million people were re-housed.

Many Soviet citizens were pleased with the progress that had been made in the 1950s and early 1960s – they could remember the hard times of the 1930s.

Source B: From a speech by Khrushchev to the Twenty-second Congress of the Communist Party, 1961

In this decade (1960s) the Soviet Union will surpass the strongest and richest capitalist country, the United States, in production per head of the population; the Soviet people's standard of living will improve substantially; everyone will live in easy circumstances.

Source C: Distribution of consumer goods in the USSR and USA, 1955 and 1966

USSR 1955	USSR 1966	USA 1966
Radios 66	171	1300
Cars 1955 — 2	1966 — 5	1966 — 398
Televisions 1955 — 4	1966 — 82	1966 — 376
Fridges 1955 — 4	1966 — 40	1966 — 293
Washing machines 1955 — 1	1966 — 77	1966 — 259
Sewing machines 1955 — 31	1966 — 151	1966 — 136

Number of each consumer good per thousand of the population

Workers did experience increases in **real wages** and saw the government spend more money on welfare services. A seven-hour working day became standard and it became easier to change jobs.

Source D: Table of industrial output in the Soviet Union, 1955 and 1966

Output	1955	1966
Oil	70.5 million tons	243 million tons
Coal	390 million tons	578 million tons
Iron	33.3 million tons	66.2 million tons
Tractors	163,000	355,000
Electricity	170 million kwh	507 million kwh

Even though the USSR had lower living standards than the West, Khrushchev was able to parade the fact that, in terms of military might and aspects of science and technology, the USA was not the world's leader. Investment in the space industry had given the USSR several firsts, including the first satellite (1957) and then the first man in space, Yuri Gagarin in 1961. There was also huge arms spending, which diverted money away from domestic developments.

Task

2. *Using the sources and the information provided, assess Khrushchev's economic policies. Copy the table below and then, using the scale of 1–5 (5 being the best), judge how successful Khrushchev was in his economic policies. In the final column explain how you arrive at your judgement.*

	How far achieved Scale 1-5	Explanation for judgement
Production of consumer goods		
Housing		
Wages		
Industrial production		
Technology		

What changes were made to agriculture?

Source A: **Khrushchev (third from the right) inspecting the maize harvest**

Khrushchev's policies

It was in the sphere of agriculture where Khrushchev experienced failures and these eventually contributed to his downfall. This was rather ironic because Khrushchev had always thought of himself as an agricultural expert.

In 1953, agricultural output in the Soviet Union was low and the livestock population was too small. Khrushchev blamed this state of affairs on the high taxes that collective farm workers had to pay and on the low prices they received for their produce. He increased prices, cancelled the debts that many collective farms owed to the government and cut taxes.

As in industry, he wanted to encourage local decision-making. The Motor Tractor Stations (MTS) of Stalin's time (see page 107) were closed and the equipment passed to the farmers. Khrushchev also encouraged the growth of maize and it was hoped that this crop would be used as cattle fodder, thus making available more grain for human consumption.

The Virgin Lands Scheme

The government began to invest more money in farm machinery and fertilisers and the ambitious Virgin Lands Scheme was begun. Khrushchev's hope was that the Soviet Union's constant problem of insufficient food production would now be solved. The scheme proposed that large areas of unused or 'virgin' land should be brought under cultivation using a large labour force and simple methods. The plan was adopted and young communists (*Komsomol*) and army conscripts were sent to Siberia and Kazakhstan to bring the new land under cultivation.

By 1956, 35.9 million hectares of virgin land had been put to use and harvests were good in the early days of the scheme.

Huge piles of grain lay in the open roads without any sort of covering. Soviet workers turned this grain by hand to help it dry. Buckets, trowels and saucepans were used in this operation. It was raining and I know that much of the crop was lost.

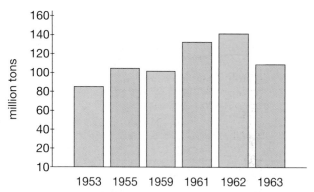

Grain production in the Soviet Union under Khrushchev, 1953–63

Task

1. *Look at Sources A and B. Explain why Khrushchev was keen to have such photographs published, not only in the Soviet Union but internationally.*

Yields from the virgin lands declined after 1958 because the land was farmed too intensively. Some crops were grown in unsuitable soils and local climate conditions were often ignored. Furthermore, there were insufficient fertilisers and in some areas there were inadequate crop drying and storage facilities. In Kazakhstan, the transport infrastructure was inefficient and crops frequently rotted after harvest (see Source C). Indeed, agriculture made little headway under Khrushchev and bad harvests in the early 1960s forced the government to raise food prices and this led to unrest in some towns and cities.

1963 proved to be a disastrous year and following hurricanes, topsoil from six million hectares was lost. In order to avoid what threatened to become a famine, large quantities of grain had to be purchased from the USA, Canada and Australia.

Tasks

2. *What problems did farmers face when Khrushchev became leader?*

3. *Why do you think that Komsomol members and soldiers were used in the initial stages of the Virgin Lands Scheme?*

4. *Write a newspaper article based on interviews with Soviet farmers in the 1950s, discussing changes in agriculture since 1930. (Look at pages 106–111 to refresh your memory about collectivisation.)*

5. *Why did Khrushchev's agricultural policies fail?*

(Remember how to answer this type of question? For further guidance see page 125).

Why did Khrushchev fall from power?

Source A: From an article by Isaac Deutscher, a British historian. He was writing in 1963 about Khrushchev's agricultural policies

Politically Khrushchev is suffering a major defeat. Even quite recently he was unwise enough to poke fun at those who had forecast soil erosion in Kazakhstan; and all these years he has walked in the glory of his success on the agricultural front. His prestige at home is shattered.

Source B: Extracts from the Communist Party Presidium meeting in October 1964 at which Khrushchev was forced to resign. The comments were made by several of the committee members

You have contradicted Lenin's teaching in agriculture and industry . . .
We now have the cult of Khrushchev . . .
You are coarse, rude, erratic and hasty . . .
You listen too much to members of your family . . .
You juggled the fate of the world over Cuba . . .
You don't pay attention to anyone and don't hear anyone out.

Developing problems for Khrushchev

There was an inkling for Khrushchev in 1962 that his policies were not running smoothly. There were riots in the city of Novocherkassk that year, when workers had objected to wage cuts and price rises. They chanted 'Use Khrushchev for sausage meat'. This was intended as a sarcastic comment, because Khrushchev had once said 'What sort of communism is it that cannot produce sausage?'. More than 80 protesters were killed in these demonstrations.

In October 1964, Khrushchev interrupted his holiday and returned to Moscow to attend a meeting of the **Presidium**. At the meeting he was sternly criticised by its members (see Source B) and was forced to resign. The reason given to the people of the Soviet Union was ill health. However, dissatisfaction with Khrushchev and his policies had been growing over several years.

The criticisms of Khrushchev

Many disliked Khrushchev for his overbearing attitude and his rough manners. He had a tendency to make decisions with little thought and considered himself an expert on most issues. He had hoped to remove the unnecessary bureaucracy of the Stalin era, but it turned out to be too ingrained to make the changes he wanted.

Khrushchev's industrial policies fell between two stools – he did not produce enough consumer goods to satisfy the population and the attempts to do so alienated some senior colleagues who felt that priority should go to heavy industry. The military withdrew their support because they believed that there should be no reduction on arms expenditure. The Virgin Lands Scheme clearly failed and it was humiliating to have to buy grain from the USA.

His forays into foreign policy were heavily criticised and the Presidium accused him of mishandling the Cuban Missiles Crisis (see photo) and, furthermore, creating a rift in relations with China.

On Khrushchev's removal, Leonid Brezhnev was appointed Secretary of the Communist Party and Alexei Kosygin became Prime Minister.

MISSILE EQUIPMENT
MARIEL PORT FACILITY
4 NOVEMBER 1962

LAUNCH STANDS

17 MISSILE ERECTORS

The Cuban Missiles Crisis happened in October 1962, when the USA and USSR almost went to war as a result of Khrushchev's decision to base nuclear weapons on Cuba. This is an aerial intelligence photograph of missile erectors and launch stands at the Mariel Port Facility in Cuba during the Crisis.

Source C: From *The Rise and Fall of the Soviet Empire* by D. Volkogonov, 1998. Volkogonov was a Soviet historian who continued to write after the collapse of the Soviet Union
It is normal for a leader to be feared or cursed or criticised, but when he is laughed at and made the butt of jokes, his time is up. After the sinister giants of Lenin and Stalin, it seems that in the end Khrushchev was somehow too lightweight for the public ... As a reformer he was not understood, while many were simply not willing to forgive him for exposing the personality cult.

Tasks

1. *Write an obituary for Khrushchev. Remember to make a balanced judgement about his life.*

2. *Explain the reasons why Khrushchev was removed. To answer, make a table as below, so that you can see those areas which proved problematic for him.*

Character	Comparisons with Stalin	Industrial problems	Agricultural problems	Foreign affairs

Examination practice

Sometimes in Section (b) on Paper 1 there will be a question similar to the following:

Question 1

Choose two items from the boxes and explain why each was important for Khrushchev as leader of the Soviet Union.

De-Stalinisation	Virgin Lands Scheme	Regional Economic Councils

(10 marks)

How to answer

- This question is always out of ten marks and each item is then marked out of five.
- Having selected the two items carefully, you should write about each one separately. Aim to write about two lengthy paragraphs.
- As in all questions, you must analyse the wording and look for the key areas.
- The topic areas are given but you must not simply write all you know about the topic. Here, the key areas are 'Khrushchev's leadership' and 'importance'.
- Naturally, you must be able to discuss each item you choose, but your answer should indicate to the examiner that you understand how the item relates to the question. For example, for the question above, how each policy enabled Khrushchev to secure his position and bring change to the Soviet Union.
- Remember to use the words of the question to ensure that your focus is clear and direct.

The following example shows you how to discuss one of the items in the box.

Example answer

The Virgin Lands Scheme was important for Khrushchev because if it was successful he would be able to tighten his grip as leader. The plan was his idea and it was huge in scale, showing the people of the Soviet Union that he was a leader with vision. The Soviet Union had not been able to produce sufficient quantities of grain and if the fear of famine could once and for all be removed then he would be seen as probably greater than Stalin.

However, after initial successes and large harvests, the scheme failed. There were more grain shortages in the early 1960s and the Soviet Union was humiliated when it had to buy stocks from the USA and Canada. The failure of the scheme resulted in not only the Party leaders criticising Khrushchev but also ordinary people.

Overall, it was a good idea but ultimately disastrous for Khrushchev's leadership because it gave ammunition to his enemies.

Now have a go yourself

Answer the question using the other two items in the box.

The decline and fall of the communist state

Tasks

The cartoon shows the hammer and sickle, the symbol of communism.

1. *What are they doing?*

2. *Why do think they are shown like this?*

Source A: **A cartoon in the *Guardian*, a British newspaper, in January 1991**

By 1992, the Soviet Union no longer existed. It had been replaced by more than 50 regions and republics. In addition, during the preceding three years, Soviet control of Eastern Europe had ended and virtually all these countries had thrown out their communist governments. The decline and fall of the Soviet Union happened very quickly, with great drama, and was mainly due to the policies of Mikhail Gorbachev, its last communist leader.

This chapter will answer the following questions:

• What were the key features of the Brezhnev years?
• Why were there leadership changes between 1982 and 1985?
• Why did the Soviet Union collapse?
• What were Gorbachev's aims and policies?
• Why did Gorbachev's policies fail?
• How did the communist state collapse?

Exam skills

There is guidance on how to answer the scaffolding question in Section (b) of Paper 1. For this question you have to write an essay worth 15 marks, the most of any question on either paper.

What were the key features of the Brezhnev years?

Leonid Brezhnev ruled the Soviet Union following the resignation of Khrushchev until his death in 1982. He reversed the process of reform that Khrushchev had started. He gave up the idea of change and for the next eighteen years the Soviet Union stagnated. It has even been suggested that, in 1976, Brezhnev had a stroke, which left him clinically dead and an invalid for the next six years.

Brezhnev's rise to power

Source A: A portrait showing Brezhnev wearing a great number of medals

Leonid Illich Brezhnev was born in Kamenskoye, Ukraine, in 1906. He became a full member of the Communist Party in 1931. He studied at the Dniprodzerhinsk Metallurgical Institute,

graduating in 1935 as an engineer and became the director of a technical school.

His career flourished under Stalin and, by 1939, he had become Secretary of the regional Party Committee at Dnipropetrovsk. During the Second World War he served as a political commissar in the Red Army and had reached the rank of major general by 1943.

After the war, he held a number of important posts and had become a member of the *Politburo* by 1952. He continued to progress under Khrushchev and, by 1960, was chairman of the Presidium of the Supreme Soviet. By 1964 he was considered as Khrushchev's heir apparent and led the coalition that forced him from power (see page 130).

Personality cult

Source B: Brezhnev and other leaders taken on a visit to the Ukraine in 1981

Over the next few years Brezhnev ensured that he became the Soviet leader. At first, he shared the leadership with Alexei Kosygin but within a few years he had emerged as the dominant figure. He became the first person in Soviet history to hold both the leadership of the Party and of the state.

He encouraged a 'personality cult' of himself, similar to the Cult of Stalin (see page 82). He had portraits, like the one in Source A, made of himself. Brezhnev's love of drink, especially vodka, flattery and being awarded medals became a source

Task

1. *Why do you think Brezhnev is wearing so many medals in Source A?*

2. *Look at Source B. Do they deserve the title of 'geriatric' leaders'?*

of jokes. During the last few years of his life, crippling illnesses certainly reduced him to a figurehead surrounded by other older people in poor health. It was said that the Soviet Union was run from the geriatric ward of the **Kremlin**.

Repression

Also, like Stalin, Brezhnev refused to tolerate opposition or criticism. In 1965, he ordered a crackdown on:

- writers and scientists who resented government control over their work
- **dissidents**
- some religious groups
- the leaders of some of the nationalities who wanted greater freedom from Soviet control.

Writers and artists

Thousands of writers and other intellectuals were arrested and some were put on trial, including Alexander Solzhenitsyn and Andrei Sakharov. The former was exiled from the USSR in 1974 for the criticisms of the USSR put forward in his book *The Gulag Archipelago* but the scientist, Sakharov, the creator of the Soviet hydrogen bomb, was not allowed to leave.

Case study: The Ukrainian mathematician, Leonid Plyushch

Plyushch was interned for two years in a psychiatric hospital in the Soviet Union. His case was tried in January 1973 and the court ruled that he was mentally ill. He had been accused of writing several 'anti-Soviet' articles, having 'anti-Soviet' conversations with several people and of signing open letters to the UN. He was sent to a psychiatric hospital for treatment. He was eventually released and allowed political asylum in the West.

Leonid Plyushch giving a press conference after his release and arrival in the West

Task

3. *How might an official Soviet newspaper have reported the trial of Leonid Plyushch? Put together the headlines for such a newspaper.*

Dissidents

Brezhnev appointed Yuri Andropov as the new head of the KGB (the secret police). He began to lock dissidents in psychiatric hospitals in an effort to break their spirit. Andropov, however, had one problem he was not able to solve. Members of Brezhnev's own family were involved in corruption, more especially the giving and taking of bribes. Brezhnev's daughter, her lover and his sons were all involved, but Andropov could not deal with them until after Brezhnev's death.

The most prominent group of dissidents was the Jews who wished to leave the Soviet Union and live in Israel. Thousands were allowed to go, but the better educated were forced to stay. They were too valuable for the country to lose.

Brezhnev's treatment of the dissidents, especially putting some into psychiatric hospitals, made him very unpopular abroad, especially in the West.

Tasks

4. *Think of three key words to summarise Brezhnev's career and policies.*

5. *In what ways did Brezhnev continue the policies of Stalin?*

(Remember how to answer this type of question? For further guidance see page 105.)

6. *Describe the key features of Brezhnev's policy of repression.*

(Remember how to answer this type of question? For further guidance see page 99.)

Problems at home

Brezhnev had little interest in domestic policies, preferring to concentrate on policies aboard. As a result, the problems of the Soviet Union, which Khrushchev had tried unsuccessfully to solve, became worse.

Brezhnev believed that much needed reform of the economy would meet with opposition from the same hard-line communists who had overthrown Khrushchev. He avoided major change at a time when the Soviet economy stagnated and there were significant shortages of consumer goods and food.

Nevertheless, there was some progress. By 1980, it was reported that:

- 85 per cent of families owned radios
- 83 per cent of families owned TV sets
- 86 per cent of families owned refrigerators
- 70 per cent of families owned washing machines
- 9 per cent of families owned cars.

Diet was also healthier with more meat, milk and vegetables and less bread and potatoes.

Farming also improved. Brezhnev encouraged the greater use of fertilizer and new farming techniques, which brought better results than under his predecessor, especially in Kazakhstan. In the friendlier atmosphere of **détente**, the Soviet Union was able to make up grain shortages with **imports** from the West. As an exporter of oil and natural gas, it benefited from the rising energy prices of the 1970s, and profits from this trade bought food and western technology.

The 'Brezhnev Doctrine'

Brezhnev's foreign policy favoured peaceful co-operation with the West, because the Soviet Union badly needed Western technology, grain and money to develop the economy. This led to a period of détente or relaxation in tension over Eastern Europe.

However, his policies abroad eventually worsened the economic problems of the Soviet Union, because his own ambitious policies frightened the West. For example, in 1968, he invaded Czechoslovakia to overthrow a reforming communist government.

This, in turn, led to the 'Brezhnev Doctrine', by which the Soviet Union claimed the right to intervene in support of any communist government, anywhere in the world. He supported this Doctrine by spending even more money on armaments and nuclear missiles, which put an even greater strain on the Soviet economy.

It was Brezhnev's decision to invade Afghanistan in 1979 that finally shattered détente. It also embroiled the Soviet Union in a very expensive, protracted war, which its economy could ill afford. The war lasted until 1989.

Source C: A cartoon in the British newspaper, *The Daily Telegraph*, 3 January 1980. Brezhnev is shown holding the hammer

THE HAMMER & CRESCENT

Tasks

7. *What message is the cartoonist trying to get across in Source C?*

8. *Describe the key features of Brezhnev's economic policies.*

(Remember how to answer this type of question? For further guidance see page 99.)

9. *Prepare a two-minute talk summarising the career and achievements of Brezhnev.*

- *What are the key areas you will have to include?*

- *How much will you be able to say about each of these?*

- *Time yourself to ensure you stick to the two-minute guideline.*

Why were there leadership changes between 1982 and 1985?

In the three years following the death of Brezhnev, the Soviet Union had two leaders, both of whom died within a short time of taking office.

Name: Yuri Andropov, 1914–84

Andropov was born in Russia in 1914 and left school at the age of eleven, holding several jobs before he entered the Komsomol or Communist Youth League (see page 84). He rose rapidly under Stalin and, by 1938, he was first secretary of the Komsomol Central Committee.

During the Second World War he took part in partisan guerrilla activities against the Germans and, in 1951, became a member of the Communist Party's Central Committee in Moscow. In 1954, he was sent as Soviet Ambassador to Hungary and it was his reports to Moscow that eventually convinced Khrushchev of the need to invade Hungary to end the uprising in 1956.

In 1962, he was promoted to the Communist Party Central Committee Secretariat and five years later became head of the KGB, the secret police. It was in this role that he really made a name for himself. He became the instrument of Brezhnev's policy of clamping down on dissidents. Andropov 'refined' the methods of the KGB to deal with dissidents. Dissidents were frequently confined to psychiatric hospitals (see page 135), whilst the most famous dissidents were 'allowed' to emigrate.

By 1973, Andropov was a full member of the Politburo and, just days after Brezhnev's death on 10 November 1982, he became the Communist Party's general secretary. He was only leader for fifteen months and had little time to achieve much. He did, however:
- *try to improve the efficiency of the economy*
- *try to persuade the Europeans not to allow the USA to station Pershing Missiles in Germany.*

He died in February 1984. Historians still debate whether he would have been a real reformer if he had lived longer.

Yuri Andropov, 1914–84

Name: Konstantin Chernenko, 1911–85

Chernenko was born the son of a peasant farmer in Siberia in 1911. He joined the Komsomol in 1929 and two years later became a member of the Communist Party. During the Second World War he worked as a party propagandist.

When, in 1952, Brezhnev became a member of the Politburo, Chernenko was appointed his personal assistant. He made little progress under Khrushchev, but his career developed again under Brezhnev's leadership. In 1971, he became a full member of the Communist Party Central Committee. Seven years later he made it into the Politburo.

He was widely regarded as Brezhnev's likely successor in 1982, but was passed over in favour of Andropov. When the latter died in 1984, Chernenko became leader, but he was dogged by ill health and died thirteen months later in March 1985, having been unable, and perhaps unwilling, to tackle the problems faced by the Soviet Union.

Konstantin Chernenko, 1911–85

Tasks

1. Why is the period 1982–85 often described as a period of stagnation in the Soviet Union?

(Remember how to answer this type of question? For further guidance see page 117.)

2. Choose either Andropov or Chernenko. Prepare a one-minute talk on their career and achievements.

The decline and fall of the communist state

Why did the Soviet Union collapse?

In 1985, Mikhail Gorbachev became leader of the Soviet Union and began a series of reforms that had huge repercussions for the Soviet Union, Eastern Europe and the Cold War.

Who was Mikhail Gorbachev?

Mikhail Gorbachev, 1931–

Gorbachev was born in 1931 in the village of Privolnoye in Stavropol province. His family were poor farmers and, at the age of thirteen, Mikhail began working on the farm. In the 1950s, he studied law at Moscow University but, after graduating, he returned to his native village, working as a Communist Party official. He was eventually promoted to the central committee of the Communist Party, with responsibility for agriculture.

At the age of only 49 he became a member of the *Politburo*, and was deputy leader during Chernenko's brief period in power, succeeding him as leader in 1985.

What problems did Gorbachev face?
Economic problems
The main problem was that the Soviet Union was trying to be a **superpower** with an economy that could not sustain this position. To pay for its foreign policy, the Soviet Union needed to make money abroad, but it had few saleable exports. Only grain and raw materials could be sold as exports, but it did not have enough grain to feed its own population.

Economic growth, so spectacular under Stalin,

fell from a high of six to seven per cent in the 1950s, to three per cent in the 1970s, and a further drop to two per cent in the early 1980s. By the mid-1980s, 24,000 of the 46,000 state enterprises were running at a loss.

In addition, Soviet manufactured goods were often of a poor quality and could not be sold to the West. This was especially true of Soviet-produced cars, such as the Lada, which were often the butt of jokes.

Question: **What do you call a Lada with a sunroof?**

Answer: A skip!

The Soviet Union was not even **self sufficient** in food. By the time of Brezhnev's death, the productivity in collective farming had reached an all-time low. Brezhnev had tried to address this problem by investing $500 billion in agriculture between 1965 and 1980. Nevertheless, grain imports in the same period cost $15 billion. In 1981–82 the gap between grain produced and the amount needed was 44 million tonnes.

Social problems
The declining economy also affected living standards. There were chronic shortages of almost everything. Every Soviet housewife faced the problem of shortages every day. Shopping in the USSR was very different from the West. First you had to find a shop that had the item you wanted in stock and then join the queue.

One result of this was a thriving underground economy. In 1985, the Soviet newspaper *Izvestia*, revealed that there was a black market for foreign consumer goods in the Soviet Union worth 7,000,000,000 roubles a year because of the shortage of consumer goods. The Soviet economy could not produce what the citizens of the USSR wanted. Consumer goods and food were scarce and queuing could take a whole day. For example, a car cost the equivalent of seven years' wages.

Moreover, the younger generation in the Soviet Union began to compare their lifestyle to that of their counterparts in the West. Brezhnev warned his colleagues about this in a speech to the Twenty-sixth Party Congress in 1981 (Source A):

> ### Source A: Brezhnev's speech to the Twenty-sixth Party Congress, 1981
>
> *The things that we are speaking of – food, consumer goods, services – are issues in the daily life of millions and millions of people. The people will judge our work in large measure by how these questions are solved. They will judge, exactly. And that, comrades, we must remember.*

Many Russian workers, depressed with their lifestyle, turned to alcohol, especially vodka. Ten per cent of workers regularly arrived for work drunk. Even worse, life expectancy in the Soviet Union had declined from 64 years old in 1964 to 62 in 1980, largely as a result of alcoholism.

The cost of the Cold War
The problems were certainly worsened by the commitments of the Soviet Union abroad. Since the 1950s, vast amounts of money had been spent trying to compete with the USA. The space race and nuclear arms race placed far too great a strain on the Soviet economy. In addition, the Soviet Union had financially supported other communist regimes in Eastern Europe and, more especially, in Cuba.

Finally, the invasion of Afghanistan (see page 136) and the subsequent struggle to keep control, was a further massive drain on Soviet finances. The cost in cash, equipment and lives was immense and turned many ordinary Soviet citizens against the government. In the 1980s, the Soviet Union was running a 35,000,000,000 rouble annual **budget deficit**.

Political stagnation
The economic problems were made worse by the political situation. Khrushchev had been the last leader to try, unsuccessfully, to tackle the Soviet Union's economic policies. His successor, Brezhnev, was less inclined to reform, in order to maintain the support of the members of the *Politburo*. Therefore, the Soviet Union stagnated during his leadership and, if anything, the economic problems worsened. His two successors, did not have the time, nor perhaps the inclination, to tackle the problems faced by the Soviet Union.

Tasks

1. Gorbachev faced economic, political, social and foreign policy problems in 1985. Show how these problems were inter-linked using either

- a Venn diagram

OR

- a concept map.

In either case, label and explain the links.

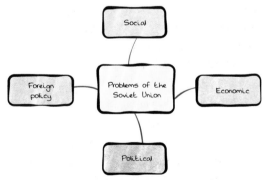

2. Why did Gorbachev face problems in the Soviet Union when be became leader in 1985?

(Remember how to answer this type of question? For further guidance see page 117.)

What were Gorbachev's aims and policies?

Gorbachev set out to confront the problems that Brezhnev had avoided. He came to power with two main aims, which were *Perestroika* and *Glasnost*.

Perestroika

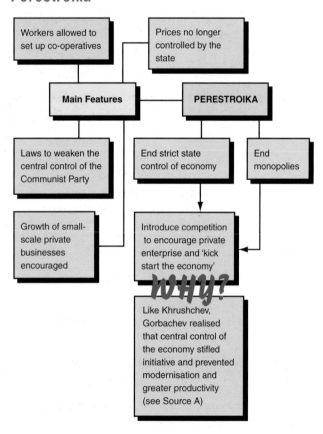

Perestroika
Economic restructuring.

Glasnost
'Openness' – both with the Soviet Union and with the West.

Source A: **Gorbachev in a speech in 1986**

Can the economy really be run by trillions of calculations from Moscow? That's absurd, comrades! And that is where the great mistake lies, in the fact that until very recently we have tried to run everything from Moscow.

Glasnost

This meant 'openness' both within the Soviet Union and with the West. Within the Soviet Union Gorbachev hoped this would encourage initiative by relaxing control over the media and arts. With the West, he had ulterior motives. He realised that the survival of the Soviet Union was dependent on the West. He needed their investment to help develop the Soviet economy. In addition, he realised that the arms race was crippling the Soviet Union. The way forward was to reach an arms agreement with the West, which would enable him to reduce the massive defence spending and, hopefully, **balance the budget**.

Censorship of the press was relaxed and Western ideas and music began to flood the Soviet Union. In 1990, the first McDonalds fast food restaurant was opened in Moscow. The Orthodox Church was allowed to practise its religion with freedom for the first time since the Bolshevik Revolution of 1917. The powers of the KGB were greatly reduced and then the KGB itself abolished. Its records were made public. The infamous Lubianka prison was closed. Gorbachev himself walked round the streets of Russian cities meeting the Russian people.

Source B: **Gorbachev and his wife, Raisa, walking round the streets of Moscow greeting the Soviet people**

Dissidents were no longer locked in psychiatric hospitals. In 1986, the leading dissident, Dr Andrei Sakharov, was released from internal exile.

The political system was reorganised, with the introduction of free elections for local government. Gorbachev adopted a policy of *demokratizatsiya* or **democratisation** and the first free elections were held in 1990. Non-communist groups were even allowed to contest elections against official Party candidates. However, Gorbachev did not want to end communist rule in the Soviet Union, but make it more effective and popular.

Gorbachev also moved quickly to put an end to the expensive and dangerous arms race.

Source C: **Gorbachev speaking in 1987**

The time is ripe for abandoning views on foreign policy, which are influenced by an imperial standpoint. Neither the Soviet Union nor the USA is able to force its will on others. It is possible to suppress, compel, bribe, break or blast but only for a certain period. We must respect one another and everybody.

In a series of face-to-face meetings with American Presidents, Reagan and Bush, he agreed to real arms reductions. To further improve relations with the West, and reduce spending, in 1989 he removed Soviet troops from Afghanistan.

Source D: **The famous meeting between Reagan and Gorbachev at Geneva, November 1985. The two men got on really well together**

Tasks

1. *Look at the diagram summarising the main aims and features of Perestroika. Use the information on Glasnost to create a similar diagram showing its main aims and features.*

2. *What can you learn from Source A about the weaknesses of the Soviet economy?*

(This is an inference question. For further guidance see page 16.)

3. *Describe the key features of Gorbachev's policies of Glasnost and Perestroika.*

(Remember how to answer this type of question? For further guidance see page 99.)

4. *What message does Source B give about Gorbachev and his wife?*

5. *Does Source D support the evidence of Source C about Gorbachev's aims in foreign policy? Explain your answer.*

(This is a cross-reference question. For further guidance see page 23.)

Why did Gorbachev's policies fail?

Gorbachev's policies did not solve the problems of the Soviet Union. It was a case of too little, too late. The problems of the economy were too great and had been building up since the 1950s. Gorbachev realised that he had to act quickly but, at the same time, any reforms would need a while to take effect. Many Soviet citizens expected immediate benefits. When this did not happen, there was opposition and chaos.

He was faced with powerful opposition from leading members of the Communist Party who resented his attempts to 'westernize' the Soviet Union and feared that he intended to destroy the position of their party. Ultimately, Gorbachev was caught between two camps – the hard-line party members who demanded an end to all reform, and reformers led by Boris Yeltsin (see page 146), who demanded even more.

The majority of Soviet people were unable or unwilling to adapt to his changes. They had been used to being told what to do and had no experience of democracy and freedom and could not cope with them.

In addition, the policy of *Glasnost*, giving people greater freedom, backfired on Gorbachev. Instead of making the Soviet people accept communism and work together, it encouraged them to ask for more. As he walked round the streets of Moscow he faced increasing criticism and even abuse.

Greater freedom also encouraged the states that made up the Soviet Union to demand self-government and independence (see photo). Indeed, *Glasnost* and *Perestroika* highlighted one of the biggest weaknesses of the Soviet Union. It was made up of numerous different peoples and nationalities, many of whom resented being controlled from Moscow and having to follow Russian customs and language.

Fundamental to the success of Gorbachev's economic policies, was much needed financial help from the West, in the form of loans and investment. He hoped that by agreeing to arms limitations, countries such as Britain, USA, France, Germany and Japan would willingly offer

Muslims demonstrating against Soviet control of Azerbaijan in 1989

financial support. He was wrong. The Western powers had no intention of rescuing his reforms. They thought that the discontent and chaos would lead to the end of communism and of Soviet control of Eastern Europe. They were right.

Tasks

Which do you think was the most important reason for the failure of Gorbachev's policies? Make a copy of the following table:

Reason for failure	Rating 1-5	Explanation

- *In the left-hand column list all the reasons.*

- *In the middle column give each reason an importance rating from 1 (Not very important) to 5 (Decisive).*

- *Give a reason for your judgement in the right-hand column.*

How did the communist state collapse?

Gorbachev's reforms brought a wave of criticisms and unrest, which surprisingly quickly brought his own downfall and the break-up of the Soviet Union.

End to Soviet control of Eastern Europe

In March 1989, Gorbachev announced that the Red Army would no longer prop up communist regimes. The countries of Eastern Europe took advantage of this as shown in the photos below and on page 144.

June 1989
In Poland, free elections were held and the first non-communist leader elected

November 1989
East Germans march to checkpoints at the Berlin Wall. The guards throw down their weapons and join the demonstrators. The Berlin Wall is taken down.

October 1989
Enormous demonstrations in East German cities when Gorbachev visits

The decline and fall of the communist state

November 1989
Huge demonstrations in Czechoslovakia, which opens its borders to the West and allows the formation of new political parties

December 1989
In Bulgaria, large-scale demonstrations against the Communist government

December 1989
In Hungary, free elections are held

December 1989
The Romanian dictator, Ceausescu, is overthrown

Task

1. *Write a series of British newspaper headlines for the events shown in the photos on page 143 and above.*

The break-up of the Soviet Union

Glasnost had encouraged independence movements in the states that made up the Soviet Union. The Baltic states of Lithuania, Estonia and Latvia were the first to demand more freedom. In 1989, Gorbachev was forced to withdraw Soviet troops from these states.

Azerbaijan was next to demand its freedom in 1990. Gorbachev sent troops to end the rioting there. In May, the Russian Republic, the largest within the USSR, elected Boris Yeltsin as speaker. Yeltsin, in turn, said that there was no future for the Soviet Union and encouraged the various states to break from it. In July, the Ukraine declared its independence and other states followed.

In January 1991, there were further riots in Lithuania and Gorbachev sent in the troops. In April, Georgia declared its independence. Gorbachev seemed to have lost control.

The fall of Gorbachev

At first, the main threat to Gorbachev seemed to come from Boris Yeltsin. In February 1991, he openly attacked Gorbachev and sparked off massive demonstrations, which forced Gorbachev to call in the troops. Eventually, however, Gorbachev backed down, leaving Yeltsin in a very strong position. This became even stronger when Yeltsin, rather than Gorbachev, persuaded Siberian coal miners, striking for greater freedom, to return to work.

However, the first strike against Gorbachev did not come from Yeltsin but from communist hardliners and military officers. In 1991, they had had enough and organised a *coup* to take over the USSR. Matters came to a head when Gorbachev organised a conference to discuss the future of the Soviet Union. Hardliners feared this might trigger the end of the Soviet Union.

The plotters included Gorbachev's prime minister, Pavlov, and the head of the armed forces, Dimitry Yazov. They struck on 2 August 1991 whilst Gorbachev was on holiday in the Crimea. They kept him prisoner in his holiday home, and tanks and troops were sent onto the streets of Moscow.

Source A: A Russian quoted in the *Independent* in August 1991

Gorbachev's an idiot. He should never have gone on holiday. They've done him just like Khrushchev.

Task

2. *What can you learn from Source A about the reasons for the* coup?

(This is an inference question. For further guidance see page 16.)

On 19 August 1991, Radio Moscow announced that Gorbachev had been replaced by Vice-president Gennady Yanayev and a **state of emergency** was declared.

Gorbachev was saved by huge crowds who gathered in opposition to the *coup*. These crowds were led by the Russian President, Boris Yeltsin, who had emerged as the leader of popular opposition.

The *coup* soon collapsed. Unable to defeat the rebellion by force and faced by defiant crowds, the *coup* leaders flew back to the Crimea to see Gorbachev. Yeltsin's supporters, however, got there first and brought him back to Moscow. Meanwhile, the leaders of the *coup* were arrested and sent to jail. At least two of the men involved committed suicide.

Source B: A famous photograph showing Boris Yeltsin talking to the crowds in Moscow from the top of a tank, August 1991. This is part of what he said:

*Citizens of Russia. On the night of the 18 August 1991, the lawfully-elected President was deposed. Let us be clear. We are dealing with a **reactionary**, unconstitutional coup. I call on the soldiers. Take no part in this reactionary coup! We call for a general strike.*

Real power now lay in the hands of Yeltsin. He was seen as the saviour of the 'revolution'. The defeat of the *coup* had not reinforced Gorbachev's authority. On the contrary, it hastened his downfall. Yeltsin humiliated Gorbachev in front of the Russian parliament, pointing out that he had chosen all the *coup* leaders himself.

The end of the Soviet Union

The failure of the *coup* meant an end to the Soviet Union. The separate states were no longer prepared to form part of the Soviet Union.

In a televised speech on 25 December 1991, Gorbachev announced the end of the Soviet Union and, lacking power and support, resigned. In 1992, the states that had made up the Soviet Union agreed to join the Commonwealth of

Biography Boris Yeltsin, 1931–

Boris Yeltsin was born in 1931 in Sverdlovsk (now Yekaterinburg), the son of a peasant farmer. His father was convicted of anti-Soviet activities in 1934 and sent to a *gulag* (labour camp). During the Second World War Yeltsin, who was thirteen, blew off the thumb and forefinger of his left hand when trying to dismantle a grenade.

He graduated from the Ural Polytechnic Institute in 1955 and joined the Communist Party six years later. Gorbachev promoted Yeltsin to the *Politburo* and, from 1985 to 1987, he was the First Secretary of the Communist Party in Moscow. He was sacked from these positions in 1987 for criticising the slow pace of reform under Gorbachev.

Within two years he had found a new opening, being elected to the **Congress of People's Deputies** and gaining a seat in the Supreme Soviet of Russia. In May 1990, he was appointed speaker of the Supreme Soviet of Russia and the following month declared Russia's independence. In the democratic presidential elections for Russia, in June 1991, Yeltsin won 57 per cent of the popular vote.

Independent States (CIS). This meant that the Soviet Union had now been replaced by a group of independent states.

The process then went even further. The Russian Confederation was made up of more than 50 autonomous regions and republics, and many of these took the opportunity to try to break away from the control of Moscow.

The Commonwealth of Independent States

Tasks

3. Why had Gorbachev lost most of his power by the end of 1991?

(Remember how to answer this type of question? For further guidance see page 117.)

4. You are a British TV reporter who witnesses the coup of August 1991, especially Yeltsin's actions. Put together a two-minute news report on the key events.

5. How will history judge Gorbachev? Draw up a balance sheet of his successes and failures.

Successes	Failures

Use your balance sheet to write a paragraph on Gorbachev for a publisher who is putting together a book of famous twentieth-century people.

Examination practice

Below is guidance on how to answer the scaffolding question. In the previous chapter you were given advice on the 10-mark question (page 125). This is the other question in Section (b) and is worth 15 marks – the most marks for any question on Papers 1 and 2. It is called the scaffolding question because the examiner not only gives you an essay type question but also four points (or scaffolding) to help you plan and write your answer.

Question 1 – scaffolding

In what ways did Gorbachev's policies bring change to the Soviet Union in the years 1985 to 1991?

You may use the following information to help you with your answer:

Perestroika
Glasnost
Eastern Europe
The break-up of the Soviet Union

(15 marks)

How to answer

- Ensure you do not simply describe the four parts of the scaffolding.
- Focus on the key words in the question. Many of these questions are about change.
- Make use of each part of the scaffolding. The examiner has often put them in a logical or chronological order.
- Do a quick plan making use of each part of the scaffolding.
- Write an introduction that identifies the key areas you intend to explain in your answer.

The steps you should take when answering a scaffolding question are shown on page 149.

Question 2 – scaffolding

In what ways did Stalin establish control over the Soviet Union in the years 1928 to 1941?

You may use the following information to help with your answer:

The 'Cult of Stalin'
The 'Show Trials'
The purges
Education

(15 marks)

Now have a go yourself

Make a copy of the following grid and use it to help you plan your answer.

Introduction

First paragraph – first scaffolding factor
Introduce the first scaffolding factor and then fully explain it. Make a judgement on how much change it brought. Make the same judgement for each factor.

Link with second factor

Second paragraph – second scaffolding factor

Link with third factor

Third paragraph – third scaffolding factor

Link with fourth factor

Fourth paragraph – fourth scaffolding factor

Link with extra factor

Fifth paragraph – fifth factor

Conclusion

STEP 1
Write an introduction which identifies the key areas you intend to explain in your answer.

Example
In his brief period as leader, Gorbachev brought about immediate and long lasting changes to the Soviet Union. In the short term, Perestroika and Glasnost attempted to change the attitudes and economy of the Soviet Union. Over the longer term, these changes, in turn, brought an end to Soviet control of eastern Europe and hastened the break up of the Soviet Union itself.

STEP 2
Write at least one good-length paragraph on each part of the scaffolding.

Begin each paragraph with a sentence that focuses on the question.

One immediate change brought about by Gorbachev was his policy of Perestroika, which meant economic structuring.

Give a developed explanation of this factor, making sure you focus on how it changed the Soviet Union.

STEP 3
Try to make links between each of the scaffolding factors. Remember the link words that you used in the ten-mark question (see page 125).

A possible link between Perestroika and Glasnost could be:

Moreover, to enable Gorbachev to bring about economic restructuring and encourage foreign investment, he introduced Glasnost, or openness which...

STEP 4
Write a good-length paragraph for each of the remaining three parts of the scaffold.

Have a go yourself

STEP 5
If you can think of one additional factor, write a paragraph on this. Make sure that the examiner is aware that this is an additional factor.

One possibility for this essay could be the fall of Gorbachev:

Gorbachev's policies, or their failure, also brought another change which was his own fall from power and the emergence of another leader, Boris Yeltsin.

You will need to give a fully developed argument about his fall from power and its impact on the Soviet Union.

STEP 6
Write a conclusion making your final judgement on the question.

Example
Gorbachev's policies brought about fundamental and long lasting changes to the Soviet Union. Glasnost and Perestroika failed in their original aims of improving the economy of the Soviet Union but did encourage even greater changes in Eastern Europe where the communist satellite states ended Soviet control. They also brought about the downfall of Gorbachev and the break up of the Soviet Union itself.

Glossary

Abdicate To give up the throne.

All-Russian Congress of Soviets A meeting of representatives from the newly created soviets.

Alliance bloc A group of countries that have agreed to help each other against rival countries or blocs.

Allied Powers Britain, France and USA.

Anarchic In a lawless state.

Armaments Military equipment.

Autocracy Rule by one person who has complete power.

Autonomous Self-government.

Balance the budget Ensure that spending matches revenue.

Bolshevik Revolution This took place October/November 1917 when the Bolsheviks seized power.

Budget deficit When a government spends more than it gets in revenue or taxes.

Buffer state A small country, often between two rival states.

Capitalism Economic system based on private ownership of the means of production, distribution and exchange.

Censorship To ban or cut parts of a newspaper, book, film etc which the government does not like.

Civil rights The political, economic and social rights of a citizen, e.g. the right to vote and equal treatment under law.

Civil war War between people of the same country.

Collective farm A farm or group of farms managed and owned through the state.

Collectivisation Process introduced by Stalin whereby individual's farms and land were put together and then run by a committee. All animals, tools and the produce of the farm were to be shared.

Comintern Short for 'Communist International' – international organisation based in Russia, formed to assist the growth of communism all over the world.

Commissar Term for government minister.

Commissar of Nationalities Minister of member of government responsible for non-Russians.

Commune A village organisation controlled by heads of families – it redistributed land and organised payment of taxes.

Congress of People's Deputies Equivalent of parliament.

Constituent Assembly Parliament.

Constitution The system of rules by which a state is ruled.

Counter-revolution A revolution that tries to reverse the results of one that has just occurred.

Coup d'état Violent or illegal change of government.

Cuban Missiles Crisis Crisis in October 1962, when the USA and USSR almost went to war as a result of Khrushchev's decision to base nuclear weapons on Cuba.

Democracy A system of governing a country, either directly by the people, or by holding regular elections to some form of parliament or assembly which makes the law.

De-Stalinisation The elimination of the influence of Stalin.

Détente A French word meaning the relaxing or easing of relations between two countries. This was the word used to describe relations between the Soviet Union and the USA in the 1970s and later 1980s.

Diplomatic isolation Many governments around the world refused to send ambassadors to the USSR and cut off all contact.

Dissident A person who disagreed with the communist policies and lack of freedom in the Soviet Union.

Elite An exclusive group or section.

Feudalism Medieval legal and social system in which people were obligated to their lord.

Five-Year Plan Set of targets for industry set by the central planning organisation, *Gosplan*.

Garrisoned Troops stationed in a fortress or barracks.

Glasnost 'Openness' – both with the Soviet Union and with the West.

Gosplan The State Planning Authority. An organisation run by the Communist Party. It was given the task of planning the industrialisation of the USSR under the Five-Year Plans. *Gosplan* set targets for industries and allocated resources.

*Gulag*s Prisons where inmates were punished by forced labour.

Haemophilia Hereditary disease that prevents the blood from clotting during bleeding. Even a minor cut could lead to excessive bleeding and death.

Hedonistic Indulging in sensual pleasures.

Icon An image of a sacred person, the icon itself is sacred.

Ideological Reflecting the ideas of a political system.

Imports The purchase of goods or services from foreign countries.

Industrialisation Process of developing key industries, especially heavy industries such as coal and iron.

Inflation A rise in prices caused by too much money and credit relative to the available goods.

KGB Name of secret police from Khrushchev to Gorbachev.

Kremlin The twelfth-century citadel in the centre of Moscow containing the offices of the Soviet government.

Kulak The name given to the better-off peasants who had benefited from Lenin's New Economic Policy. From selling their produce, these peasants became more well-off than other peasants and began to employ poorer peasants to work for them.

Land reform Changing methods of farming and assisting peasants with loans.

Liberal party A political party which follows ideas based on individual freedom and tolerance.

'Little father' Phrase used by Russians to describe the tsar.

Marxism The thoughts of Karl Marx who was the founder of communism.

Menshevik A member of one of the groups formed after the split in the Social Democratic Party in 1903. They believed the Party should be a mass organisation, which all workers could join.

Military dictatorship Rule by the armed forces.

Military Revolutionary Committee (MRC) A body originally set up by Social Revolutionaries and the Social Democrats to defend against Germany and counter-revolution.

Mutinied Soldiers rebelled against their officers.

Narodniks The Russian word for people. A revolutionary group grew up in the late nineteenth century using this word as its name.

NATO North Atlantic Treaty Organisation set up in 1949 by the USA and Canada and countries in Western Europe as a defensive alliance to prevent the spread of communism.

New Economic Policy Introduced in 1921 by Lenin to win back support of people. Allowed private businesses and farms and profit.

NKVD Name of secret police under Stalin.

OGPU The state security force which succeeded the Cheka (the Bolshevik secret police).

Old Bolsheviks Original Bolshevik Party members under Lenin.

Oratorical Public speaking.

Orthodox Church Branch of Christianity, strong in Eastern Europe, established by a breakaway from the Catholic Church in the early middle ages.

Pact Agreement.

Partisan A civilian who carries on fighting against an enemy occupying their country in wartime.

Perestroika Economic restructuring.

Persecution To mistreat an individual or group because of their race and/or religion.

Politburo The policy-making committee of the Communist Party in the Soviet Union.

Pravda The official Communist Party newspaper.

Presidium Term used for Politburo.

Protector The rulers of Russia had influence in Eastern Europe and 'looked after' the interests of nationalities in this area.

Provisional Committee A temporary body set up until there could be a permanent government established.

Purge The systematic removal of enemies through terror.

Reactionary Someone totally opposed to reform.

Real wages The value of what money earned can buy in relation to the value of goods.

Red Army The Soviet army.

Red Guard The Bolsheviks' own armed forces.

Requisitioning Seizing produce.

Revolution A sudden and drastic change in a society's political, economic or cultural structures. Marx's view of a revolution was a violent overthrow of one system of production to the next – e.g. capitalism to socialism.

Right wing In this case, the less extreme communists who were prepared to accept some capitalist ideas.

Romanov dynasty Romanov was the family name of tsar Nicholas. His family had ruled Russia since 1613.

Saboteur A person who deliberately destructs property.

Satellite state A state under the control of another country.

Self-sufficient When a country can produce enough for its own needs and does not need to import from abroad.

Serf A person attached to the land and the property of the landowner.

Shock brigades Groups of workers who were selected or volunteered for especially arduous tasks.

Socialism The belief that all means of production should be owned and run by the government for the benefit of everyone and that wealth should be divided equally.

Socialist Believer in the idea that there should be state ownership and control of the means of production, distribution and exchange.

Socialist state A state in which everyone has an equal opportunity to benefit from the country's wealth, usually by having the main industries owned by the state.

Soviet An elected council of workers.

Spring Offensive The last major German attack on the Western Front.

Stakhanovites Followers of Alexei Stakhanov – a miner, who, in the 1930s, had moved 102 tons of coal in one shift – who were dedicated to hard work.

State of emergency Condition declared by a government in which martial law applies.

Subsistence farming Producing just enough to live on with little or nothing left over to sell.

Superpower The name given to the two most powerful nations in the world, the Soviet Union and USA, in the years after 1945.

Supreme Soviet Soviets were local and regional workers' councils. Representatives from the regional soviets were sent to the central or Supreme Soviet.

Terror Stalin's purges of the 1930s.

Testament Will.

Totalitarian state A state in which those in power control every aspect of people's lives.

Triple Entente Agreements made between Britain, France and Russia in 1907.

Utopian communist state A state where citizens work freely for the sake of everyone else, using his/her own ability to the best advantage of society.

Warsaw Pact A military alliance of eight nations set up in 1956 by the Soviet Union to counter the threat from NATO.

World socialist revolution Lenin and Trotsky thought the Bolshevik Revolution would inspire workers all over the world to rebel against their governments and set up socialist states.

Answer to task 2, page 77: Yezhov was purged by Stalin in 1938. This, in itself, is very strange as Yezhov was the Chief of the Secret Police responsible for carrying out many of Stalin's purges. After he was purged the picture was altered to remove him.

Index